Weather

W*eather*

L*ouise* Q*uayle*

CRESCENT BOOKS
NEW YORK

A FRIEDMAN GROUP BOOK

This 1990 edition published by Crescent Books
distributed by Crown Publishers, Inc.
225 Park Avenue South
New York, NY 10003

ISBN 0-517-67663-X

Weather
was prepared and produced by
Michael Friedman Publishing Group, Inc.
15 West 26th Street
New York, New York 10010

Editor: Sharyn Rosart
Designer / Illustrator: Mary Moriarty
Photography Editor: Christopher Bain
Photo Researcher: Daniella Jo Nilva
Production: Karen L. Greenberg

Color Separation by Universal Colour Scanning, Ltd.
Printed and bound in Hong Kong by Leefung-Asco Printers Ltd.

h g f e d c b a

Dedication

To Dad, an inveterate weather watcher, on the links and off

Acknowledgments

Thanks to Allan Margolin of the Environmental Defense Fund and to James Howcroft of the National Meteorological Center for their help with research. And, of course, many thanks to Robin Nagle for editing portions of the text, and for her invaluable advice on breathing.

CONTENTS

Introduction

The weather probably has captured more public attention in recent years than it has at any other time. The severe storms of the 1970s, droughts of the 1980s, evidence of a melting Antarctic ice cap, and holes in the ozone lead many to believe that the weather is a sign of massive changes to come in the climate of our planet. Some sound an urgent alarm: The greenhouse effect is upon us and all our efforts to reduce the amount of pollutants in our air, water, and land won't stem the tides of change. Just as earth's climate has changed time and again over the millennia, so another radical change may now be occurring: We are witnesses, but it is beyond our control. We may even have set in motion a sequence of weather events that will lead to the extinction of the human race.

From the beginning, humans have celebrated and wondered about the intricate chain of events that creates, destroys, and recreates our rain and snow, the spectacular atmospheric lights, and the power of hurricanes and tornadoes. While our understanding of these phenomena has grown over the last century, and has improved vastly in the past twenty to thirty years, still they remain something of a mystery, even to scientists. This book explains what we know about the earth's weather: how it is shaped by the atmosphere, oceans, and land; what impact our celestial neighbors have on weather cycles; how rainbows and other atmospheric phenomena dance with light to reflect colors in the sky; and what long-term influence humans may have on our changing climate.

The history of our fascination with the weather is a long one. Our ancestors in the east and west, from Asia to Africa and Europe to South America, left a record in art, myth, and legend that reflects their own concerns with the weather. More than one creation myth begins with the marriage of the god of the sky and the goddess of the earth. Their children became the gods and goddesses that ruled the seasonal rains, the fires in the sky, and the fury of storms. In ancient pagan cultures the earth itself was worshiped as the goddess Gaia. In Asia one myth explained that the earth rested inside a blue sapphire. The sun reflected the sapphire's color and made the sky blue. Sprinkled throughout *Weather* are other myths and legends that humans have created to explain various weather phenomena.

The influence weather has on us doesn't end with myth and religion. Countless songs, paintings, and poems pay tribute to the joys of spring and the ravages of winter storms. Who can forget Gene Kelly's happy-go-lucky spring dance in *Singin' in the Rain* or that classic tune comparing love's confusion to a stormy day, "Stormy Weather?"

When we're not pondering the weather's relationship to our emotions, we do keep close track of it on a day-to-day basis. The Weather Channel broadcasts national and international weather news nationwide. Americans make one billion calls to weather-information numbers every year at a cost of about $100 million. We spend another $100 million on radios that broadcast weather predictions from the National Oceanographic and Atmospheric Administration. The weather has also become an important part of the regular television news program. Every year commercial television spends about $500 million producing weather reports.

Our abiding interest in the weather reflects the profound effect it has on all aspects of our lives. Some studies show that the weather actually affects the way we feel, emotionally and physically. Areas of low pressure may cause a period of low feelings for some people. SAD, or Seasonal Affective Disorder, is a form of depression that affects some people only in winter, when they receive less sunlight.

Today our awareness of weather's effect on us is further heightened by the recent indications that there may be major changes already occurring in our weather. We are deluded if we think we can separate ourselves from nature for very much longer; some ask if we have betrayed the planet, others if we are betraying ourselves.

As you enjoy the photographs and illustrations throughout this book, I hope you'll regard the processes that make the weather happen with as much wonder as I have. They truly are something to celebrate. Yet this book is more that a colorful meditation on the beauty of earth's complex systems. The more we learn about how our weather works, the more we can do to heal the wounds we have inflicted on the earth. Pretty pictures may have a calming effect, but as you look, think about the ways in which every one of us contributes to the land, sea, and atmosphere. How can we, on a local and personal level, work toward environmental sanity? Chapter Seven outlines some of the harmful chemicals and pollutants that we use in industry and at home and suggests alternatives for a healthier planet. At the back of the book is a list of environmental groups. Donate to, or better yet, volunteer for one. Encourage your neighbors to participate in existing recycling programs or start one if none exist in your area. Consider the amount of carbon dioxide that your car dumps into the atmosphere—about one ton for each ton of car—the next time you drive two blocks that you could walk.

With *Weather* in hand you can understand something about the fragile niche humans fill in the global scheme, learn to anticipate your local weather, marvel at photographs of rarely seen phenomena, and experience some of the more spectacular events the weather has to offer.

Snow, brought by the cold, harsh winds of the polar jet stream, blankets some areas of North America from September through May.

The Blue Bubble

There is something fascinating about science. One gets such wholesale returns of conjecture out of such trifling investment of fact.

— Mark Twain

THOUGH WE'VE GROWN ACCUSTOMED TO CERTAIN CONSTANTS ABOUT THE WEATHER—IT RAINS IN THE SPRING AND SNOWS IN THE WINTER—EARTH'S WEATHER HAS CHANGED MANY TIMES SINCE THE EARTH FIRST TOOK SHAPE FOUR AND A HALF BILLION YEARS AGO. HUMANITY'S 750,000-YEAR TENURE HERE IS REALLY QUITE SHORT. A SERIES OF INTERACTIONS BETWEEN EARTH AND ITS ATMOSPHERE LED TO THE WEATHER WE KNOW TODAY. THE COMBINA-TION OF VOLCANIC ACTIVITY, EARTHQUAKES AND PLATE TECTONICS, THE OCEANS, THE ATMOSPHERE, AND THE INFLUENCE OF EARTH'S MAGNETIC FIELD AND RADIATION FROM THE SUN ALL CONTRIBUTE TO THE STORY OF EARTH'S CLIMATE.

tudy of these interrelated forces takes the discipline of many different sciences. Geologists, paleoclimatologists, oceanographers, and other earth-oriented scientists, as well as physicists, paleontologists, chemists, and biochemists, all grapple with the questions of how the earth was first formed and how it continually redefines itself.

Averaging the effects of weather over a period of years defines the earth's overall climate. Based on what they know of earth's history, scientists speculate that our climate is gradually changing (see Chapter Seven), just as it has been for billions of years. The history of earth is revealed to us when we learn to understand its atmosphere, the fossil record, the movement of the continents, and the influence of earth's magnetic field in combination with the earth's tilt toward the sun and the effects of the sun's radiation and magnetism on earth.

As light waves pass through the water and other particles in the sky, seemingly endless variations appear in the sky's color spectrum.

THE ATMOSPHERE

When the earth was first formed, the composition of the elements in the atmosphere was quite different from that of today. Scientists believe that all the basic ingredients were there—methane, carbon dioxide, water vapor, hydrogen, and ammonia—but these hadn't mixed to form the atmosphere as we know it. It took 800 million years of "chemical evolution" to create the atmosphere around earth. Simple molecules were bombarded with energy from the sun and lightning and with chemicals, ash, and energy from hydrothermal and volcanic activity beneath the earth's surface.

Volcanic eruptions spewed nitrogen, carbon dioxide, sulfur dioxide, hydrogen sulfide, water vapor, and other trace elements into the atmosphere. Along with these elements, tons of ash and debris floated into the atmosphere, creating huge clouds that became electrically charged. Energy from lightning and the heat and chemicals produced in the volcanic eruptions reacted with the simple elements in the atmosphere. These reactions eventually led to the development of the first single-cell organisms, which appeared on earth about four billion years ago. Yet the atmosphere as we know it probably didn't appear until the Cambrian period, some 580 million years ago.

Earth's climate continued to change dramatically, warming and cooling in neverending cycles. For millions of years, glaciers advanced and retreated across the oceans and continents, carving out valleys and rivers; volcanoes dispersed chemicals and

Particles emitted during volcanic eruptions helped form the atmosphere as we know it today. From modern observations of eruptions we know that ash and particles travel high into the atmosphere where winds carry them thousands of miles around the globe, adding color to sunsets and affecting weather in some places.

ash into the atmosphere; and earthquakes shifted huge land masses across vast oceans. It took many years for scientists to correlate their studies of changes in the earth's orbit around the sun, the fossil record, and earth's changing magnetism to understand when and how the movement of continents and glaciations occurred. By looking at the relationships between these factors in earth's history, scientists can better understand the changes in the earth's climate over the billions of years of its existence.

17

Proxies of Recent Climate Change

Our knowledge of earth's recent climate history is nearly as sketchy as that of ancient climate history. Detailed weather records have been kept for little more than one hundred years. To compensate for the dearth of weather records in humankind's short history, scientists read the story of the effects of gradual climate change on our ancestors through some unusual and creative means called proxies.

One period from 1645 to 1850 has particularly fascinated climate historians. During this time, Europe and the Northeastern United States experienced a period of harsh, cold winters. Known as the Little Ice Age, its existence has been supported by sources as diverse as records from French wineries, which show a poor grape harvest because of the cold, and accounts of Revolutionary War cannons being transported across a frozen Long Island Sound. Paintings of frozen Dutch canals by seventeenth-century artists like Frans Hals, Rembrandt van Rijn, and Jan Vermeer were once thought to be fantastical, fictional representations. Yet shipping records from the period show that the canals actually did freeze during seventeen winters.

Graveyards offer another sort of proxy. Greenland's Norse settlers arrived there about one thousand years ago. By studying the condition of their graves and analyzing the remains in them, scientists know that Greenland is no misnomer. It once was green; it froze about five hundred years ago.

The "Great Snow" of 1717 covered colonial New England during what is now known as the Little Ice Age. Artists' drawings are just one of the many "proxies" scientists use to determine what the weather was like hundreds of years ago before weather records were kept.

Huge glaciers advanced and retreated over the earth's surface as its climate changed time and again throughout its 4.5 billion-year history.

EARTH CYCLES

Little more than a century and a half ago scientists began to suspect that a series of ice ages, in which much of the earth was covered with ice, and the activity of volcanoes and earthquakes had to do with changing climate. As little as twenty years ago, data from the relatively new sciences of geology and glaciology were analyzed to begin unraveling earth's mysteries.

During the first half of the nineteenth century, scientists in Europe sought to explain the presence of huge "misfit boulders," or erratic blocks, in valleys where they did not match the surrounding rock. The Swiss naturalist Louis Agassiz, founder of the science of glaciology, was the first researcher to convince the scientific community that glaciers might once have covered the continent of Europe and carved out its mountains and rivers when they receded.

In all, scientists believe that there have been five glacial epochs, within which shorter ice ages occurred. In the last two million years, they believe the ice has come twenty times. A period of advancing ice is called a glaciation, which lasts about one hundred thousand years. Interspersed with these cold periods, warmer conditions prevailed for ten-thousand-year intervals. These shorter, warmer periods are known as interglacials. The current interglacial has lasted about nine thousand years.

Until recently, dating rocks and fossils was an imprecise science. With the advent of radioactive isotope dating in the 1940s, however, scientists had a tool with which they could more accurately calculate the age and climate conditions in which rocks and fossils were formed.

Much of what we know about the formation of earth and its climate lies buried in layers of rock and sediment beneath land and sea. By studying fossils and layers of sediment known as varve, scientists can determine what the earth's climate was like during various periods in earth's history. These layers show that the earth has undergone many periods of warming and cooling. In studies of small marine fossils, scientists analyze the ratio of oxygen 16 to oxygen 18 to determine what the average water temperature was at the time and thus what the climate was like. Those shell fossils low in oxygen 16 reflect a period of general cooling because the advancing glaciers absorb the oxygen 16; conversely, when the ice retreats, the level of oxygen 16 in the water rises. This occurs because oxygen 16 is lighter and leaves the surface more readily than oxygen 18. As oxygen 16 collects in the atmosphere, it will, over time, create the clouds and conditions for the cooling of the earth.

These samples drawn from beneath the ocean floor tell the story of five hundred thousand years of earth's history. Based on the fossil study, scientists showed in 1976 that ice-age cycles occurred at 100,000, 43,000, 24,000, and 19,500 years.

Sky Cycles

Long before the science of geology was developed, astronomers noted that changing weather patterns correlated with changes in the earth's position in the solar system. While geologists perfected their understanding of the earth's history based on the age and make-up of rocks and fossils, astronomers studied the changing position of the sun in the sky and cycles in the earth's orbit.

The Greek astronomer Hipparchus (150 B.C.) noted that the point where the sun reaches its equinox changes 1.5 degrees every century, completing a full cycle every twenty-six thousand years. This is called the precession of the equinoxes. In 1842, about the same time that Agassiz proposed his theory of glaciation, the French mathematician Joseph Alphonse Adhemar estimated that the climate would change every eleven thousand years, when the earth was at the farthest possible point from the sun. He believed the earth's climate changed because of the tilt of its axis and its elliptical orbit around the sun.

In 1911, the Yugoslavian scientist Milutin Milankovitch resolved to settle the question of the ice ages and the earth's climate cycles. Milankovitch calculated that there had been three ice-age cycles 100,000, 41,000, and 22,000 years ago. He based his calculations on how variations in the earth's orbit around the sun would change the amount of sunlight reaching earth; the 92,000-year cycle of earth's orbit, in which it becomes more elliptical, reducing the amount of solar energy absorbed by the earth; and on the changes in the angle of tilt of the earth's axis, which varies between 22.1 and 24.5 degrees every 40,000 years.

Though Milankovitch's cycles don't exactly match those found in the fossil record, the two are close enough for scientists to determine the earth's climate cycles, give or take a few thousand years. The geologic record also supports Milankovitch's theory, which predated the earth scientists' discoveries by nearly forty years.

Astronomers have studied the sun's changing position in the sky for thousands of years. They learned to recognize the change in seasons from year to year and, later, the effect of earth's orbit around the sun on earth's overall climate in cycles that last thousands of years.

MAGNETISM

E arth's magnetic field also tells us something about its climate history. Magnetic north is the point that helps us find our way with a compass. Sailors, who rely on compasses for navigation, have long noted slight changes in the direction the needle points. The earth's magnetism moves slightly every year, gradually moving around the globe. Scientists believe that the earth's magnetism, sometimes shifts dramatically, flipping from the Northern Hemisphere to the Southern Hemisphere.

Geologists have documented these changes in the earth's magnetism by studying the lineup of iron compounds in rocks. Depending on where the rock is found and the direction the iron compounds face, scientists can tell where the North Pole was when the rock formed. Through studying the differences in rocks from layer to layer in areas from South Africa to India and from Iceland to the northwestern United States, scientists have discovered that for the past 80 million years, magnetic reversals have occurred every five hundred thousand years. It seems we are overdue for a magnetic reversal because the placement of the current magnetic field has lasted seven hundred thousand years.

Changes in the geomagnetic field can have a huge impact on the earth's climate. The field deflects cosmic radiation; if the field were to reverse, the theory goes, ionization in the atmosphere would increase, creating more clouds and blocking the warmth of the sun. Without the sun's warmth, ice would cover the planet and droughts would be widespread as the

amount of free water decreased. Some scientists believe that changes in the magnetic field led directly to mass extinctions (as with the dinosaurs 65 million years ago) while others argue that the climate change would have been gradual and that the extinctions are merely coincidental.

At a conference on global catastrophes held in 1988 in Snowbird, Utah, scientists from the Lawrence Berkeley Laboratory of the University of California proposed that magnetic reversals result from the impact of huge asteroids falling to earth. These scientists say that vast amounts of dust and debris were thrown into the atmosphere, creating cooling at the poles. With more ice and snow at the poles, sea levels at the lower latitudes dropped, shifting the distribution of the earth's mass and speeding up its rotation. With the increase in rotation, the distribution of the earth's magnetism changed.

Though this is a fascinating theory, scientists still don't agree on why the magnetism shifts or what effects it would have on the weather.

Some scientists believe that droughts, such as the one in California's Sonoma Valley in 1988, signal changes in earth's climate. Change in the earth's magnetic field is one "feedback" scientists study to understand how earth's climate has changed in the past and to predict how it will change in the future.

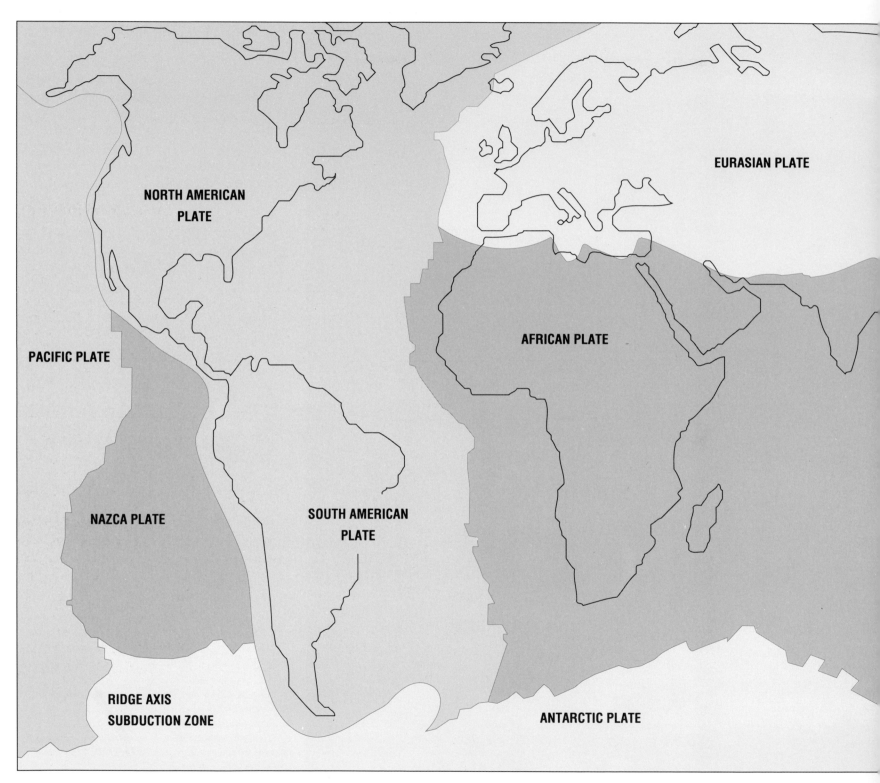

NORTH AMERICAN
PLATE

EURASIAN PLATE

PACIFIC PLATE

AFRICAN PLATE

NAZCA PLATE

SOUTH AMERICAN
PLATE

RIDGE AXIS
SUBDUCTION ZONE

ANTARCTIC PLATE

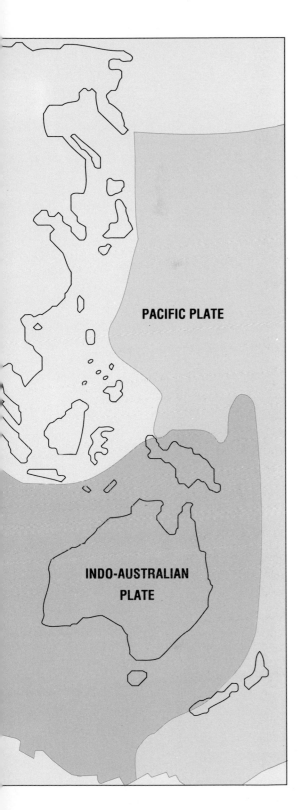

PACIFIC PLATE

INDO-AUSTRALIAN PLATE

PLATE TECTONICS

Supporting the theory of earth's changing magnetism, oceanographers discovered magnetic strips on the ocean floor in the 1960s. This discovery supported another important theory concerning the earth's history known as plate tectonics. First proposed by German scientist Alfred Wegener in 1915, the theory depicts earth's present continents as one huge land mass two hundred million years ago. He believed that over time this huge chunk of land split apart, forming the continents. Paleontologists found this an attractive theory since it helped explain the appearance of similar species thousands of miles apart on separate continents. Geologists supported plate tectonics based on similarities in rock formations.

The shifting land masses on earth contribute an important key to understanding our changing weather. The ratio and position of land to sea directly affects weather patterns, as we will discuss later in Chapters Two and Three. (See also Chapter Seven on computer models of changing weather patterns.)

The earth's crust is still moving and changing. It is divided into huge plates that move with upwelling and downpulling currents. On land, we experience shifts in the crust every time we feel the rumble of an earthquake. Beneath the ocean floor, heat creates convection currents that are described by Louise Young, author of several books on the earth, as rising "like a bubble in a kettle of thick soup." The ocean floor expands and at the same time destroys itself. As the bubbles of hot magma push up and out, they cool and sink again, pulling down more layers. These areas are known as subduction zones, where there are huge cracks and trenches in earth.

Though scientists don't exactly understand how plate tectonics, magnetism, and the interaction of earth, sea, and atmosphere have shaped the planet, their knowledge of its climate cycles leaves them with one certainty: The only constant in earth's climate is change. The earth reveals its history slowly as science pieces together the work of many disciplines to come up with an accurate scenario for earth's climate history. Today, scientists use sophisticated computer models to analyze what conditions might have been like millions of years ago. These same models may help them answer the questions surrounding our future climate patterns.

The earth's crust is divided into huge plates that constantly move, changing the shape of the continents. According to plate tectonic theory, water surrounded one giant land mass called Pangaea approximately 200 million years ago. The location and ratio of land to water directly affects weather patterns.

Earth, Air, Fire, and Water

Earth is made up of the fundamental elements of earth, air, fire, and water, which constantly exchange energy to shape the soil, the sea, the wind, and the weather. The land and oceans affect the bubble we call the atmosphere as much as the atmosphere, in turn, shapes the planet. Yet this closed system isn't as insular as we might think.

Many like to think of our global home as a self-contained living and breathing unit. We are residents of the "blue planet," our aura shining brightly in the vast, dark space surrounding us. Throughout history, humans have believed that the earth plays a unique role in the universe. From the time of Pythagoras until the work of Copernicus during the sixteenth century, we were convinced that earth revolved at the center of the solar system. Yet without the sun, the earth would be a dark satellite. The energy exchange between the sun and our planet's air, water, and earth shapes our daily weather patterns. To understand how weather happens, we must look first to the fluctuations in the sun's radiation and how the water, air, and soil react.

28

Land and sea draw energy from the sun and exchange moisture in the vast weather web. Humans have learned to harness some of nature's power in developing agricultural techniques, but the forces of earth, air, fire, and water can never be completely controlled.

FIRE

The earth's weather is shaped by the sun. Streams of charged particles, the solar wind, hurtle toward earth at a rate of 220 to 500 miles (350 to 800km) per second, reaching our atmosphere in an astonishing three-and-a-half days. Light waves from the sun create earth's blue aura, and radiation from the sun helps shape our global climate. As Louise Young, author of *Earth's Aura*, describes it, "Earth's aura does not come to an end with the last tenuous gases of its atmosphere.... In fact, no dividing line can be drawn between the aura of the sun and that of the earth—they flow together, bending and shaping each other."

Streams of hydrogen ions create a sort of electric current that circles the planet, with electrons moving west to east, and protons moving east to west. Some of the charged particles flowing away from the sun never reach earth's atmosphere and move back and forth between the earth and the sun in the Van Allen Belts. Two of these belts hover over the equator some 2,000 to 4,000 miles (3,200 to 6,400 km) and 12,000 to 18,000 miles (19,200 to 28,800 km) away. Sometimes, when the sun's energy is weakest on the dark side of earth, some of these particles escape and are drawn into the ionosphere where they collide with earth's atmospheric ions and generate tremendous amounts of energy. This phenomenon generates static-filled radio transmissions or the magnificent sky lights known as aurora australis and aurora borealis.

When the activity of these microscopic ions is high, they put on a spectacular display of light, and we see the sun's energy come to life. Every day, however, we see the sun's light and feel its energy as it heats the lands and seas of earth from dawn to dusk, season to season. The earth's orbit around the sun, the moon's orbit around earth, and the rotation of the earth on its axis all influence the angle at which the sun hits the earth's surface, creating the four seasons and our daily weather patterns.

Sunspots are another solar activity that influences our weather. A student of Aristotle's, Theophrastus of Athens, first noted sunspots in 300 B.C., but his observations received little attention. The Greeks believed the earth was the center of the solar system, and the sun embodied the power of a god; it was perfection, the fire at the center of the universe. Elsewhere in the ancient world, Chinese records showed 112 sunspot periods between 28 B.C. and A.D. 1638.

During the mid-nineteenth century, an amateur German astronomer named Heinrich Schwabe brought sunspot cycles once more to the attention of Western science. He noted that sunspot activity waxes and wanes in eleven-year cycles. Throughout history, observers have correlated weather patterns with these cycles. One controversy that scientists discuss even today deals with the Little Ice Age (1615–1715). During this period astronomers made little or no note of sunspot activity; nor did they note coronas, the bands of flame that appear during a lunar eclipse of the sun. This period of low sunspot activity has been dubbed the Maunder Minimum and has been used to prove that sunspot activity directly affects the weather.

While this "proof" of the sun's influence may at first appear conclusive, some scientists caution that the proof is only statistical. These numbers lose their significance when we remember that in the span of geologic time our records show only a small fraction of the sun's influence on the earth. How much evidence is enough? As physicist James Trefil points out, if we flip a coin ten times and it comes up heads each time, does that prove the coin has two heads? Another stumbling block in our understanding of sunspot activity is that it wasn't until the last century that frequent and sophisticated observations were made. Not only are our astronomical records limited, but the conditions under which they were kept were not always optimal for pure science. Sunspots were sometimes considered omens. In China, for example, sunspots were thought to be a sign from the heavens that the political tide was shifting. They could foretell the end of a dynasty.

Carbon 14 levels in trees fluctuate with sunspot activity. Tree-ring dating in the Pacific Northwest of the United States supports the theory that an ebb in sunspot activity has an influence on the earth's weather. Large amounts of carbon 14 in tree rings correspond to periods of low solar activity. Some scientists estimate that as little as a two percent decrease in solar radiation, such as the one experienced during the Maunder Minimum, can cause drought conditions and radically affect the earth's climate.

Whether or not sunspots have a direct effect on weather, the sun does play a featured role in other aspects of our weather

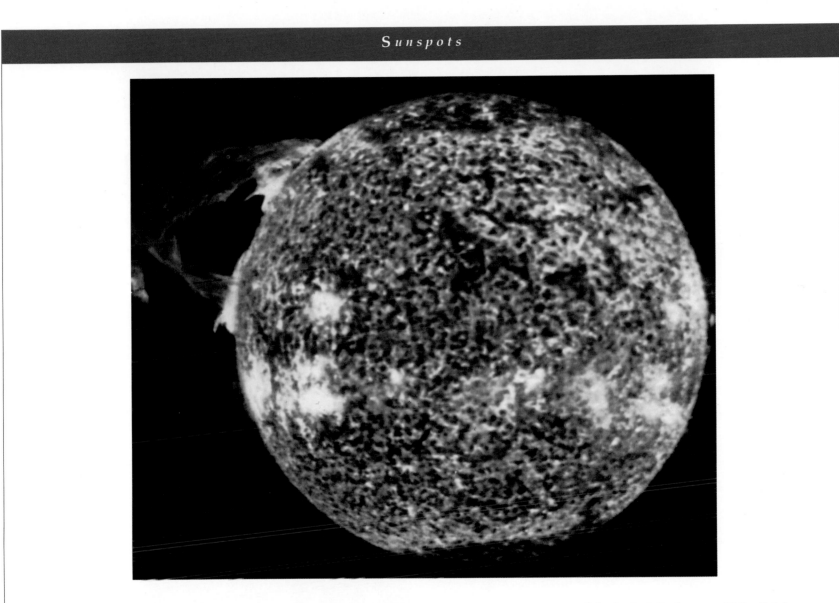

The temperatures of the sun are unimaginable. The surface of the sun is approximately 6,000°F (3,000°C). The dark spots that appear every eleven years are much cooler—about 4,000°F (2,200°C). Plasma—the mixture of positive and negative electrical charges at the sun's surface—moves around the sun in magnetic waves. When heated material from the sun's interior is prevented from bubbling to the surface by a strong magnetic field, sunspots appear.

Sunspots have been held responsible for many earthly events. During the eighteenth century, the astronomer William Herschel believed a flagging grain market could be attributed to high sunspot activity, and in A.D. 807, the spots were seen as an omen of the death of Charlemagne. While slightly more scientific calculations linked highs in sunspot activity to lower air pressure in India, lower temperatures in Scotland, and higher rainfall depths in the Great Lakes, none of these theories have held up to scientific scrutiny. Records simply haven't been kept long enough to definitely correlate sunspot cycles with these kinds of weather patterns. To illustrate the dangers of relying solely on this kind of statistical analysis, physicist James Trefil charted the rise and fall of women's hemlines. The result? They rose and fell with two cycles of the sun.

patterns. In combination with the earth's rotation, the sun is responsible for creating both wind and storms.

The sun plays a role in creating wind because it warms the planet unevenly, with the equatorial regions receiving more heat than the poles. As the sun heats the tropics, the warm air from this region rises and moves towards the poles, where it cools and sinks once again. Rising and falling masses of warm and cool air create the wind as warm air moves to equalize the cold air. Without the wind to redistribute the warm air, the sun's heat would make the tropics unbearably warm while leaving the poles frigid. Rain would fall constantly over the oceans while the land remained dry.

When the sun warms the tropical ocean, the air fills with moisture that rises and creates cumulonimbus, or storm, clouds. These storms move west and generate energy in the atmosphere, pushing up to the tropopause where the warm air is then moved by the winds toward the poles.

The wind does not flow directly to the poles because the rotation of earth causes the wind to curve west to east in the Northern Hemisphere and east to west in the Southern Hemisphere. This is known as the Coriolis effect. Heat from the sun, reflected heat from earth's surface, and the Coriolis effect are the building blocks of earth's patterns.

Left: The "northern lights," or aurora borealis, light up the night sky in the Northern Hemisphere when particles from the sun enter the thermosphere or ionosphere.

Masses of air turn to the east in the Northern Hemisphere and to the west in the Southern Hemisphere because of the earth's rotation. This illustration (right) shows the principle behind this phenomenon, which is known as the Coriolis effect. The vertical arrows show the path from which the wind is turned.

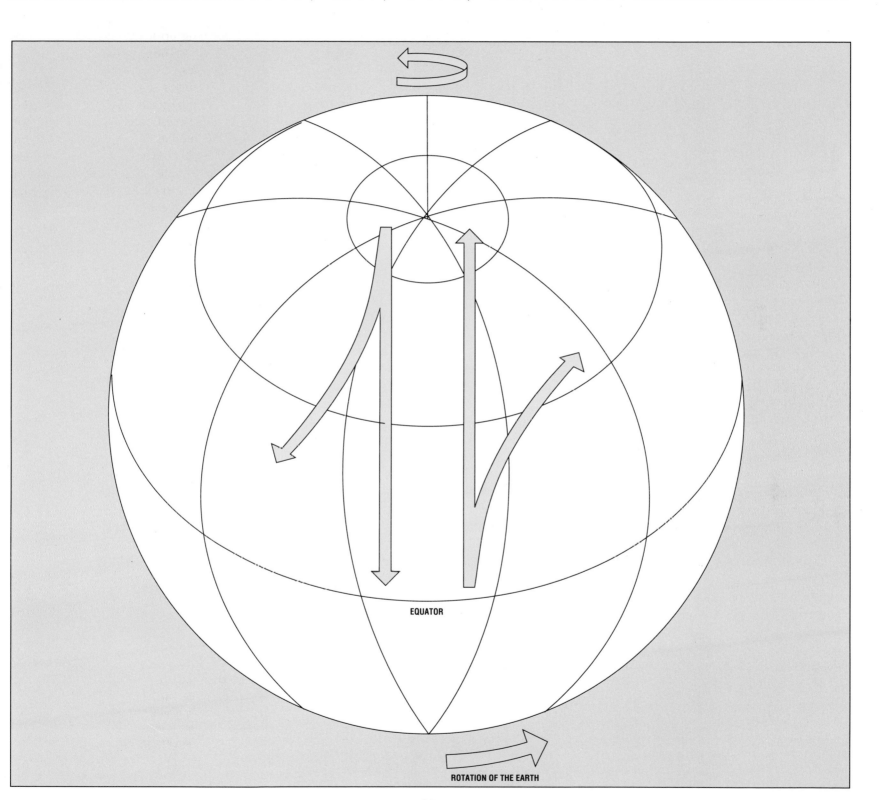

EQUATOR

ROTATION OF THE EARTH

33

AIR

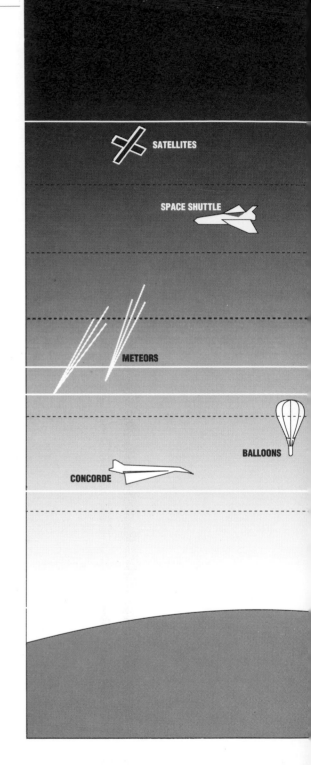

SATELLITES

SPACE SHUTTLE

METEORS

BALLOONS

CONCORDE

Earth's atmosphere weighs some five thousand million million tons and exerts pressure on humans at about fifteen pounds per square inch. Though the atmosphere reaches 18,000 miles (10,800km) up from the earth's surface, its thickness has been compared to the skin of an orange. The troposphere, the lowest layer of the atmosphere, where our weather occurs, has been likened to the skin of an apple.

Air is composed primarily of the stable gases nitrogen (78 percent), oxygen (21 percent), argon, and carbon dioxide; other gases in air include neon, helium, methane, krypton, hydrogen, nitrous oxide, and xenon. The outer reaches of the atmosphere contain less stable gases like ozone and radon.

The first layer of the atmosphere, the troposphere, derives from the Greek word *tropos,* meaning to turn or mix. This turbulent layer, the first five to ten miles (up to 18km) of atmosphere, is where most of earth's weather takes place. The temperature in the troposphere decreases with altitude and at the tropopause, the boundary between the troposphere and the next layer, the temperature drops even more. Above this, the roiling troposphere is blanketed with another layer called the stratosphere, from the Greek word meaning to smooth out. Reaching as far as thirty miles (48km) above the earth's surface, the high winds in this layer blow horizontally, carrying dust, volcanic ash, and acid rain thousands of miles around the globe. The winds are dry and clouds rare. Here, a high concentration of ozone warms the atmosphere by trapping the reflected heat from the earth. As we climb higher toward the blackness of space, the temperature increases at the lower boundaries of the mesosphere (reaching from fifteen to fifty miles [24 to 80 km] above earth) and then cools as the altitude increases. Here objects such as meteors falling to earth burn and disintegrate. Fifty miles (80km) and more above earth, temperatures in the thermosphere rise again. Within this layer is the ionosphere, where the aurorae occur. Above this layer lies the exosphere (about 250 miles [400 km] above the surface), where the earth's atmosphere eventually blends into cold, black space.

Air is constantly moving—warm air rises from the earth to the atmosphere and cool air descends from above to be warmed by the earth and sun. Even at night we can see this motion when we look at the stars. When we see them twinkle we actually are watching these currents of air move about as they balance the earth's temperature. The circulation of air is affected by land, the oceans, the sun, gravity, and the rotation of the earth. The interplay of these forces creates the effects we know as weather.

Flowing air pockets of high and low pressure, which meteorologists call cells, constantly vie with each other to equalize the earth's temperature. These cells have invisible yet distinct borders, with high pressure areas always moving toward low pressure areas.

High pressure areas generally offer clear skies with good weather; the air is stable. Two areas of earth are noted for their high pressure: the polar zones and the horse lati-

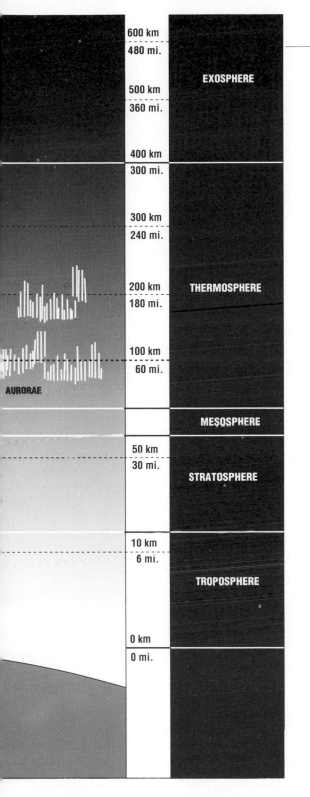

600 km
480 mi.

EXOSPHERE

500 km
360 mi.

400 km

300 mi.

THERMOSPHERE

300 km
240 mi.

200 km
180 mi.

100 km
60 mi.

AURORAE

MESOSPHERE

50 km
30 mi.

STRATOSPHERE

10 km
6 mi.

TROPOSPHERE

0 km

0 mi.

Composed of many layers, earth's atmosphere reaches hundreds of miles toward space. Most clouds form in the lowest layer, called the troposphere.

tudes (twenty-five to thirty-five degrees north and south of the equator). At the poles, high pressure forms because cool air compresses and sinks toward the surface of earth, pushing the wind toward the equator. In the horse latitudes, the sun constantly warms the oceans. As water vapor warms, rises, and is condensed out over the equator, the air becomes dense and falls back to earth as it is warmed by compression, and the amount of humidity in the air drops. Deserts like the Sahara, Arabian, Kalahari, the southwestern desert of the United States, and the Great Victoria Desert in Australia are located in these latitudes.

High and low pressure areas are sometimes called cyclones, from the Greek *kyk-loein* meaning to circle around, whirl. In the Northern Hemisphere, high pressure areas (called anticyclones) rotate clockwise while low pressure areas (called cyclones) rotate counterclockwise. When a high and low pressure system meet, the air becomes very turbulent, swirling around in an attempt to equalize the temperature.

These pockets of air circulate according to a process known as convection. During the eighteenth century, George Hadley identified the global circulation of convection cells over the Northern and Southern hemispheres. Convection transfers energy from one place to another—in the case of pockets of air, they warm and rise until they

Why the Sky is Blue

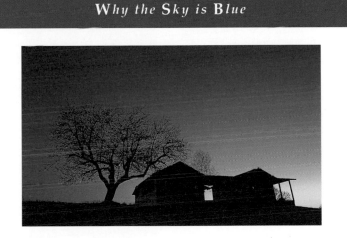

What exactly do we see when we look at the sky? Sight, of course, depends on the amount of reflected light reaching our eyes. The white light of the sun contains all the colors of the spectrum—red, orange, yellow, green, blue, and violet. As physicist James Trefil explains it, when a light beam hits the atoms in the atmosphere, the energy from the light waves is transferred to these atoms. Some of the light is reflected, or goes into the atoms in the sky, while the rest is refracted and the path it travels changes. The blue end of the spectrum—the highest in energy—is scattered by the atmosphere, making the sky blue. The sun is yellow because all of the blue has been scattered by the atmosphere. As the sun sets, more and more blue is winnowed out because light beams travel through more of the atmosphere, and the sky takes on a reddish hue. Clouds, on the other hand, appear white because the light passing through the water droplets is scattered equally—the droplets send out the same colors that come in.

reach the same density of the air to which they have risen (the inversion layer). At this point the cooled air will fall back toward earth around a rising column of warm air. The rising pockets of warm air are known as thermals. Some of the energy created by convection rises and is carried around the globe by wind tunnels called jet streams.

Much of what we know about the weather was discovered during the world wars with the advent of high-altitude flying. During World War II, the jet stream was a military secret first used by the Japanese to launch bomb-carrying balloons across five thousand miles of ocean to the United States. (Although nine hundred of the nine thousand balloons reached America, none of them caused any harm.) American pilots discovered the winds that carried these balloons across the Pacific with their first high-altitude bombing mission. At altitudes of between 27,000 and 30,000 feet (about 8,438 and 9,375m), the bombers encountered unbelievably strong winds.

Six to thirty miles (10 to 48km) above the earth's surface, where warm and cold air masses meet along the edge of the tropopause, seven jet streams circle the globe. These tunnels of air are massive—several hundred miles wide and two to three miles deep. At the outer edges of the streams, the air travels about fifty miles (80km) per hour; at the center the pace quickens to as much as three hundred miles (480km) per hour. Despite their power and speed, they travel silently because, unlike air closer to the surface, they aren't obstructed by any objects; the air at these altitudes also is thinner, thus reducing the energy of the wind.

Jet streams are located at breaks in the tropopause from thirty to thirty-five degrees in the horse latitudes and from fifty-five to

Below: Ice acts as an insulator, trapping heat at its lowest layer, and as a reflector, reflecting heat from the sun away from its surface. The warming winds of spring break up the ice. Above: The wind creates ripples in the sand and piles it in dunes, which in some places move inches every year.

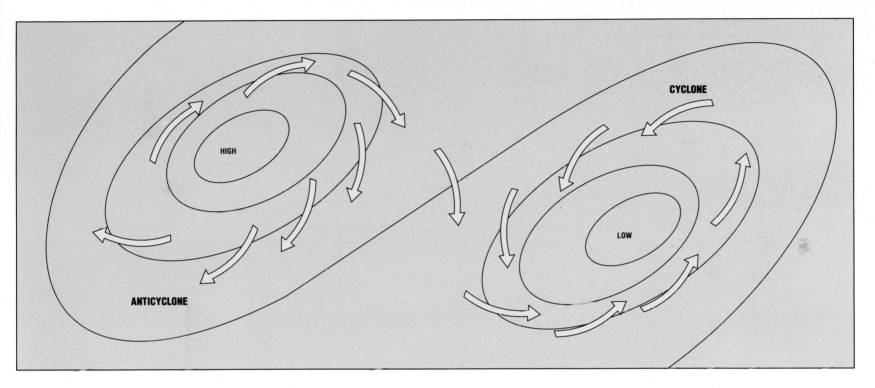

Weather is created as huge masses of air flow into each other. In the Northern Hemisphere, high pressure systems (anticyclones) rotate clockwise and generally bring clear skies and good weather. Low pressure systems (cyclones) rotate counterclockwise and are associated with clouds, rain, and bad weather.

sixty degrees where the polar air mass begins. The four jet streams that most affect our weather are the polar-front jet, the subtropical jet, the polar-night jet, and the easterly jet.

The polar-front jet flows west to east about seven miles up. It follows changes in the temperature of the upper air as the temperature rises and falls over the continents and oceans. This stream brings colder weather to North America in the winter and moves slightly north during the summer. When the speed of the jet increases, air flows out of its stream and the air below it drops in pressure. This creates a cyclone (low-pressure area) near the ground. High pressure, an anticyclone, is created below the jet stream where it slows down and air

flows back into it. Throughout the process, the jet stream pushes the systems of highs and lows eastward.

Between the mid-latitudes and the tropics, the subtropical jet plays a similar role, but only during the winter when the temperature difference between the equator and the poles is greatest. This stream is higher than the polar-front jet because the tropopause reaches higher into the sky in that region, about ten miles above the earth. Likewise, the Southern Hemisphere has two jet streams that correspond to the polar-front jet and the subtropical jet.

Two more jet streams appear seasonally as a result of the greater difference in temperatures between the poles and the equator. During the winter, the polar-night

jet appears twenty to thirty miles (32 to 48km) high while an easterly jet appears during the summer, reversing the flow of the disappearing subtropical jet streams. Over southern Asia and Africa, the easterly jet creates the monsoons of the Northern Hemisphere and is the only jet stream that flows east to west.

While tracking the movement of the jet streams may offer a sort of global thermometer because of their relationship to the exchange of heat from the tropics to the poles, water is the fundamental element in the earth's atmosphere that distinguishes ours from all the other planets in the solar system. Nearly all of the earth's weather phenomena are caused by water in one form or another.

In the tropics, the sun heats the ocean and creates frequent afternoon thunderstorms.

WATER

An instinctive recognition of the fundamental importance of water flows deep within all of us. Many people hold water sacred. They are baptized in it; they pour it over their heads at sunrise; they touch it to their foreheads in prayer. The pleasure of watching waves break on a sandy shore or listening to the rain on the roof is not just sensual. It is as reassuring as the presence of a mother is to her child. Water is there, providing our nourishment, cleansing our bodies, wrapping us in a cool, misty embrace, and singing a lullaby of a time long ago when all life was cradled in the sea.

In this passage from *Earth's Aura*, Louise Young captures the material and spiritual importance of water. In the weather equation, water is the most important variable. Water occurs in the atmosphere in three different forms—gas (water vapor), liquid, and solid (ice). In its gaseous state, water permeates the atmosphere. Water droplets are so small that fifty billion of them wouldn't fill a teacup. In its liquid form, water covers 70 percent of the earth, the oceans holding an unimaginable 48 billion billion cubic feet of it. Scientists believe that most of the water in our oceans and atmosphere has been circulating in the earth's system since its inception. The oceans and the atmosphere constantly exchange water as it moves from its gaseous to its liquid to its frozen state. Water absorbs and loses heat slowly, so the oceans moderate the global climate. Two

Tiny water particles in the atmosphere collect to form rain clouds. The droplets in the cloud collide and coalesce to form rain drops or ice crystals. When the droplets become big enough, 1/125-inch or larger, they fall to earth in the form of rain, ice, or snow. Here, rain bursts from a cloud heavy with droplets.

remarkable features of water are its low density—as vapor it is lighter than air—and its habit of expanding when it freezes. Ice is less dense than liquid water, and serves as an insulator over its liquid counterpart.

Though only one thousandth of one percent of the earth's available water is present in the atmosphere at any time, this small percentage is largely responsible for the weather we experience from day to day. Warm air holds more water vapor than cold air. As the temperature of air increases, so too does the amount of water it can hold.

When the temperature drops, the water vapor condenses into a liquid. When warmed, water vapor rises, and the atmospheric pressure around the water molecules decreases; then it expands and cools, releasing heat energy again and again, climbing even higher into the sky. If it continues to rise and cool, the water vapor will condense into droplets—forming rain, ice, or snow.

Two indicators of the weather conditions produced by water vapor in the atmosphere are the barometric pressure and the relative humidity. As warming and cooling air rises and falls, so too does its density and pressure. Barometric readings reveal the air pressure—the weight of a column of air above any particular point. When the pressure is low, we know the air is full of moisture because water vapor weighs less than air. Relative humidity expresses the amount of water vapor that the air holds as a percentage of the maximum amount the air could hold at that temperature.

With all of this water evaporating and circulating, why don't the oceans simply evaporate away? We might wonder if rain and other precipitation can resupply the oceans quickly enough. Oceanographers have discovered that underwater hydrothermal vents, or rifts, constantly push chemical compounds into the water that change the composition of the water and the floor beneath it. This activity stabilizes the water and slows its rate of evaporation.

Water droplets in the atmosphere also form fog. At night, fog is created when enough moisture in the air is cooled and condenses at the dew point. As the sun rises, the air above the water warms to a temperature higher than the dew point, causing the fog to dissipate.

EARTH

Though soil absorbs and loses heat much more rapidly than water, it plays a role similar to water in affecting weather conditions around the globe. Climatologists classify climates by similarities in the exchange of heat, moisture and air masses in various parts of the world. Though these classifications reflect similarities in the zones' weather conditions from season to season, they also say something about the land there and what it can yield.

In a system developed by British climatologist W. G. Kendrew, the continents are subdivided into geographic climate regions, each reflecting the influence of different air masses. There are four major classifications—the equatorial and tropical air masses; the tropical and polar air masses; the polar and arctic-type air masses; and the highland climates. Within each of these, further subdivisions identify regional differences in average annual weather patterns.

The rainy tropics, monsoon tropics, wet-and-dry tropics, tropical arid climate, and the tropical semi-arid climate all fall under the influence of equatorial and tropical air masses. Each of these areas experiences warm temperatures, but, with the exception of the tropical semi-arid climate, seasonal changes are less pronounced than in other climates.

In the rainy tropics, changes in temperature from day to night are barely noticeable, and year-round the temperature and humidity are high. The monsoon tropics experience the same conditions, but every winter there

The vegetation in a given area reflects the general climate profile for that region. In Indonesia (left), rice paddies thrive in the warm, moist climate of the rainy tropics. In the western United States (above), the mid-latitude semiarid climate prevails, resulting in low humidity and a hot, dry landscape in summer and a cold, snow-covered landscape in winter.

is a definite dry season until spring comes and the easterly jet pours water over Vietnam, the northern Philippines, the western Guinea coast of Africa, the northeastern coast of South America, and the northern coasts of Haiti and Puerto Rico. The wet-and-dry tropics have a two- to four-month long dry winter, receive less rainfall than the rainy tropics, and the difference between day and nighttime temperatures is greater.

Residents of North America are most familiar with the tropical arid and semiarid climates. A tropical arid climate is a desert climate—the humidity is low, the land is dry, and what little rain does fall evaporates quickly. Northwestern Mexico and the southwestern American desert fall into this category as do parts of southwestern Asia from Arabia to Pakistan, the west coast of southern Africa, and central Australia. Surrounding these desert areas are semiarid climates, mostly along the west coasts of the continents from lower California to Chile and along the northwest and southwest African coast. The warm temperatures of semiarid climates are tempered by cool ocean currents and moisture comes in the form of advection fog (see page 55), stable stratus clouds, and drizzle.

The tropical and polar air masses create the dry summer subtropics, humid subtropics, marine climate, mid-latitude arid and semiarid climates, and the humid continental warm summer and cool summer climates. The dry summer and humid subtropics are west and east coast counterparts. On the west coasts of lands in the lower middle latitudes, the stable air of the dry summer subtropics prevails, offering little rain in the summer and high temperatures. On the east coasts at these latitudes, summertime temperatures resemble those of the rainy tropics, and the air is unstable and moist. In the dry summer climates, katabatic, or gravity winds, such as the Santa Ana of Southern California, push warm air down from the mountains during the winter, often creating devastating fires. The marine climate, also on the west coasts of continents but closer to the poles, experiences wet, mild winters and comfortable summers cooled by ocean breezes. Although violent storms such as tornadoes or hurricanes are rare in northern latitudes, in the southern latitudes they do experience tremendous wind storms, giving them the name the "roaring forties," because of their degree of latitude.

Bordering on tropical climates, the mid-latitude arid and semiarid climates cover the Great Plains of the western United States and Canada, the southern portion of Russia, northern China, and western and southern Argentina. These regions are hot in the summer because of the tropical air mass and cold in the winter under the full effects of the polar air mass. Precipitation in this climate is extremely variable so any agriculture in these areas must rely on irrigation. These areas also experience the effects of warm winter winds such as the chinook in the Great Plains.

The humid continental warm summer and cool summer climates are the last two climate types to fall under the influence of both tropical and polar air masses. The humid continental warm summer climate appears only in the Northern Hemisphere because the ocean covers the corresponding latitudes in the Southern Hemisphere. Dubbed "the battleground of polar and tropical air masses," winters are cold and summers are very hot. In the United States, the Corn Belt falls into this area. In the winter, temperatures can drop from 59°F (15°C) to -4°F (-20°C) in just a day or two; in the summer, the days and nights are hot and moist from rainfall and thunderstorms. Just north of the warm summer climate, the humid continental cool summer climate, as its name implies, has a shorter growing season during its cool summers. The cool summer climate is found across the American-Canadian border from Alberta to New

Much of western Alaska falls within the taiga climate. Here the polar air mass keeps the air stable, cold, and dry.

England, in eastern Europe, and in Far East Asia.

The polar and arctic-type air masses produce the severe climates of the taiga, tundra, and the polar climates. The taiga and tundra climates are named for the vegetation in these areas. "Taiga" comes from Russian and refers to the forested areas of North America and Eurasia, which are also called the subarctic or boreal forests. The tundra appears north of the taiga on the arctic coasts of North America and Eurasia. Contrary to what we might think, the tundra is actually somewhat milder than the taiga. Arctic ice keeps the temperature slightly warmer in the tundra, but even so the average annual temperature falls below 32°F (0°

C). The polar climate is the most brutal of all. It covers Greenland, the Arctic Ocean, and Antarctica, where no vegetation grows and winter temperatures range from -4°F (-20°C) to colder than -85°F (-65°C).

Unlike any of the other climate classifications, the highland climate is defined by altitude, the local topography, and the effect of the mountains on weather. The Sierra Nevadas and Rocky Mountains in North America, the Andes in South America, the Alps in Europe, the Himalayas of Asia, the Eastern Highlands of Africa, and the mountains of Borneo and New Guinea all fall into this category. Each experiences a different microclimate based on the effects of their particular terrain on wind, but generally the

temperature drops about 43°F (23°C) with every increase of about 312 feet (100m) in altitude. The air atop these mountains is freer of clouds, dust, and smoke.

Though scientists have organized weather trends into these general climate zones, we know from experience that an area's daily weather patterns often vary from the norm. How can we explain the freak cold snap in the spring or the unusual warm spell in the dead of winter? Every day weather affects the food we eat, the clothes we wear, and the route we take to work. Even so, many weather phenomena continue to elude our logical, ordered grasp. We have yet to fully understand nature's inimitable tapestry of exchange between life's elements.

The Daily Weather

In our modern lives—insulated by cars and buildings with central air—we often take the weather for granted until it enters our lives with the force of a blizzard, the blaze of a heat wave, or the boom and crash of a thunderstorm. All over the world, the daily weather affects farmers' crops, a caravan's journey across the desert, a skier's vacation in Denver, a lunchtime walk through the park. One day we may be singing in the rain of a warm April shower and the next cursing the gray downpour that never seems to end.

In Chapter Two we saw that wind and water react with warmth from the sun to create our global weather patterns. Our daily weather is created by the same process as areas of high and low pressure move over us. Clouds form as water condenses, and rain, snow, and hail may fall.

WIND

The wind is one of the first harbingers of weather to come. In the northeastern United States, early farmers and fishermen quickly realized that the wind normally came from the west and, if it brought rain, the storm would pass mildly. In mountain areas such as the Alps in France and the Rockies and Sierra Nevadas in the western United States, residents coined special names for the warm winter winds that sweep through the mountains. Estimates are that close to 130 names have been given to such winds from region to region, from the landlash of Scotland to the _matsukoza_ of Japan, the song of the pines.

In the Southern Hemisphere, changes in the westward trade winds periodically create havoc by _not_ causing a storm. For example, sometimes the trade winds off the coast of Peru die. Normally, the water here is cooled from springs from the floor of the continental shelf. When the winds stop, the water warms to temperatures far above average, killing phytoplankton and driving off anchovies, the mainstay of Peruvian fishing. Ironically, this phenomenon is called _El Niño_, the child, because these conditions usually occur just before Christmas. When El Niño strikes, the trade winds stop or are reversed, and the warm waters off the coast of Asia move back toward the Americas. When the warm waters heat the air above, the winds are unlikely to start up for a long time.

In a phenomenon known as teleconnection, weather in one part of the globe affects weather far away in another part of

the world. In its 1982 appearance, El Niño created violent storms in Ecuador, Bolivia, and Brazil. Peru suffered flash floods and mud slides, and desert areas received as much as twelve feet of rain. At the same time, Tahiti, normally an island that doesn't experience typhoons, was ravaged by several; drought in Africa and Australia caused a severe dust storm that coated Melbourne in a soil film. Though scientists don't know if the warm waters affect the winds or the winds affect the warm waters, they do know that air pressure over the South Pacific and Indian oceans correspond. Discovered by Sir Gilbert Walker, a British mathematician, during the 1920s, the southern oscillation means that when the Indian Ocean is covered by low pressure, the South Pacific will experience a high pressure system. Yet this still doesn't explain why the winds shift. Several theories have been suggested, but no conclusions can be drawn.

Sometimes wind lashes the sea into a roiling cauldron with wave heights that made early sailors think demons were beneath them. Despite our image of the rough and wild oceans, the land actually gives more fuel to the wind than does the sea. The winds of the North Pole, for example, are less severe than the fifty-mile-per-hour winds of the Antarctic. This is because the waters of the Arctic Ocean keep things calm. Wind over other land masses is calmer than the Antarctic wind because most of the land on earth—about 80 percent—is near enough to an ocean to receive its calming influence. Also, vegetation exchanges heat with the ocean and atmo-

Farmers in the plains states of the midwestern United States depended on the windmill to predict the weather.

> **Fair Weather Tidings**
>
> When the wind is in the north,
> The skillful fisher goes not forth;
> When the wind is in the east,
> 'Tis good for neither man nor beast;
> When the wind is in the south,
> It blows the flies in the fish's mouth;
> But when the wind is in the west,
> There it is the very best.
>
> —*American folk poem*

sphere to create milder breezes. One hundred feet into a forest, the wind's power is limited by 20 to 40 percent, and as much as 90 percent of the wind's force is reduced after traveling four hundred feet into a forest. Mountains also serve as natural barriers to approaching storms.

At high altitudes the weather turns quickly from fair to foul because the wind is not blocked by protective vegetation or trees. In areas where the sea is many thousands of miles away, the temperature can rise and fall rapidly because land heats and cools more quickly than water. As winds come into contact with objects such as mountains, a wave pattern is produced, much like water flowing over an object in a river. (These lee waves create the perfect conditions for glider pilots who ride their crests for hours on end.) The wind is forced up and over the mountain, but its path isn't smooth or steady. When the air ascends the mountain it is forced into an area of lower pressure where water droplets in the air may condense to form a cloud. As the air moves down the other side of the mountain, the air pressure changes again and the cloud will disperse as it is pulled down.

Magic Bags of Wind

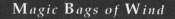

A ccording to Greek mythology, the king of the winds was Aeolus. When Odysseus sailed to Aeolus's island, Aeolus took a shine to him and gave him bags full of the violent winds that could have harmed Odysseus on his trip home. When Odysseus set sail, his sailors, either curious about what was in the bags or looking for gold, opened them, unleashing the fury of stormy winds.

Sometimes, lens-shaped (lenticular) clouds form over the top of the mountain and seem to remain fixed there. The water molecules in these clouds actively move about as the wind moves through the cloud, taking some water molecules with it and leaving others behind.

In mountainous areas, lenticular clouds sometimes signal dramatic changes in the weather. These ominous lenticular clouds in the Alps are harbingers of a hot, dry wind that screeches down the mountains during the winter. Known as the *foehn*, it quickly can raise the temperature as much as forty degrees, melting snow and threatening avalanches. The foehn is so dry, it can spark a fire, a fact that Southern Californians know from their own version of this type of wind, the Santa Ana, which flows over Los Angeles. These warm winds, a threat to some areas, can be a blessing in others. In northwestern Canada and Montana, the winter chinook brings warm relief over the Rockies to the frigid, snow-covered plains.

Winds that blow through the valleys of mountain ranges sometimes wreak havoc with cold. The *mistral* sweeps through the Rhone Valley in France, dumping cold air on Provence. In South America, the *williwaw* rages through the mountains north of Cape Horn, bringing hazardous winds to ships in the Strait of Magellan.

The deserts are another environment constantly shaped and reshaped by the wind. Wind pushes sand dunes a few inches downwind every day and heaps them together in mounds called *seifs*, which can stretch across the desert for one hundred miles and reach the height of a twenty-story building.

At high speeds, wind sweeping over the desert will create deadly sandstorms. In

areas that feel the effects of desert heat, windstorms have been described as "a burning breath from the mouth of hell," and in Turkey wind storms are called fever winds. Arabia, Turkey, and Iran all experience these warm windstorms, which often come in the form of sandstorms, spreading dust, sand, and debris everywhere.

Dust storms are by far the most common desert phenomenon. In its most severe form in North Africa, it is called the *scirocco*. Air rises as it is heated by the sand and carries small dust particles away from the surface. If temperatures are very warm, the air-borne dust particles may produce a "dry fog," which blocks the sun and reduces visibility. Sometimes the dust is carried so high that it is carried as far away as Barbados. When the scirocco blows over the Mediterranean, it may sprinkle Europe with a fine, reddish dust.

Wind and sand can be a deadly combination. Top: A sandstorm picks up momentum as the wind whips up more loose soil. In the Sahara (bottom) date palms thrive in areas with more moisture, even amongst the dry dunes that dominate the desert.

Blood Rain

In 582, Parisians were terrified when the mighty scirocco swept across the Sahara and over Europe bringing tons of red sand. It was described as a "shower of blood," which the populace was convinced had been sent down upon them as a punishment for their sins.

CLOUDS AND FOG

Clouds are by far the most common tools amateur weather-watchers use to predict the weather. Rain, snow, and hail are created when masses of cold and warm air collide. The clouds can tell us in which direction those masses are moving. Though meteorologists have identified hundreds of cloud types, there are three basic types with two qualifying terms. The names of the three basic cloud types tell us something about the stability of the air: cumulus, from the Latin for heap or pile; stratus, meaning layer; and cirrus, meaning curl. These identify the shape and formation of clouds. Nimbus, meaning rain, and alto, meaning high, give us an idea of what weather the three cloud types might produce. The piled up, puffy appearance of cumulus clouds means that the air is filled with rising air currents; stratus clouds indicate a mass of air moving over an area; and cirrus clouds appear when a large, warm air mass is rising over a cold air mass.

A cloud will form when air, warmed by the sun, starts to rise. As the air rises, the temperature and pressure around the pocket of air drops. The air cools and condensation occurs because the air can no longer hold as much water. That is the point when cloud droplets form and a cloud begins to take shape.

In a particular area, clouds will begin to form at the same altitude, known as the invection layer, the point at which the pressure and temperature can no longer hold the water molecules and condensation occurs.

All clouds form when water vapor condenses at the right temperature and pressure. Variations in the stability of the air create the three different types of clouds. Clouds form when two air masses meet. A warm, low pressure area moves in on a cooler, high pressure area.

Cirrus clouds, those feathery streaks that seem to float slowly across a blue sky, are harbingers of a coming low pressure system. Reaching six to nine miles (10 to 14km) into the sky, cirrus clouds can move as fast as one hundred miles (160km) per hour. Cirrus clouds often are on the front edge of a low pressure system, five hundred to six hundred miles (800 to 1000km) ahead of an impending storm. As the low pressure system advances, strong updrafts push pockets full of water vapor into the air, which crystallizes the water vapor and forms cirrus clouds.

Following cirrus clouds, a stable layer of stratus clouds may move in. These flat clouds form when warmer, low-pressure air flows uniformly over the colder air mass—the clouds form as the warm air mass is pushed over the cold air mass. While stratus clouds may produce rain, it is the slow, steady, long-lasting drizzle of showers rather than the violent, sometimes short-lived power of a thunderstorm.

Cumulus clouds are filled with energy and indicate that the air is very unstable. When these clouds form, the difference between the temperature and pressure of the two meeting air masses is at its greatest. As the warm air meets the cold, strong updrafts reach skyward. Water gives up heat as it condenses, which lifts the column of

Cirrus clouds above often mean a storm is coming. Composed entirely of ice crystals, they race across the sky as far as 500 miles (800km) ahead of the storm.

The two-volume International Cloud Atlas *lists the hundreds of possible cloud formations in the sky. Here, shattered cumulus clouds dot the skyscape.*

Billow clouds, a type of altocumulus cloud, streak the sky.

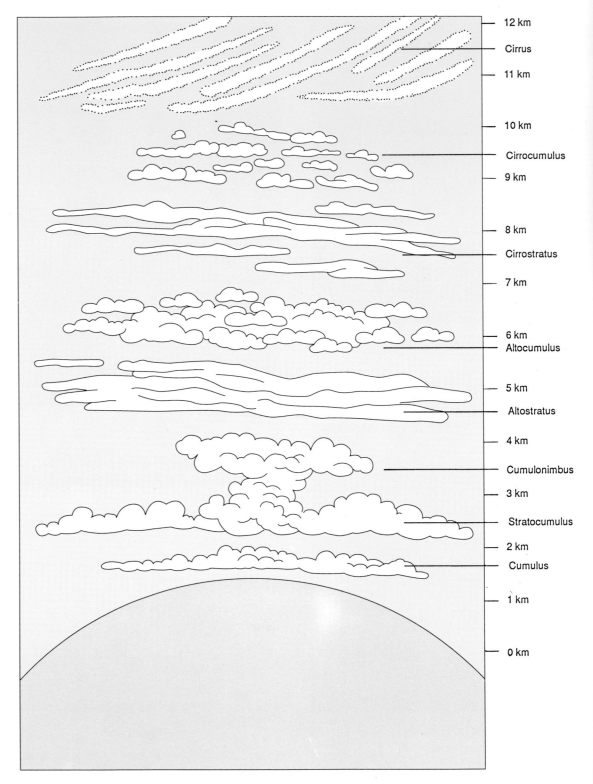

This atmospheric cross-section shows the three zones in which clouds form. Close to the earth where air conditions are likely to be more turbulent, cumulus clouds may form. When cumulus clouds spread out, they form stratocumulus clouds. Above this layer, altostratus and altocumulus clouds appear. Still higher, wispy cirrus clouds form from five to nine miles (8 to 14km) above the ground.

The Cloud

I am the daughter of Earth and Water,
And the nursling of the sky;
I pass through pores of oceans and shores;
I change, but I cannot die.

—*Percy Bysshe Shelley*

air higher and higher in the process. As Louise Young describes cumulus clouds, they look like "egg-white meringue beaten from the clear viscous medium of the earth's atmosphere into white froth and scattered on the winds." Most of us describe cumulus clouds as "cotton balls" floating in the sky. However, appearances can be deceiving. The conditions that lead to the rising and descending air that forms cumulus clouds can become charged with electrical energy and rain fire upon us in the form of lightning. Cumulonimbus clouds also can be unpredictable as cold air rushes down from them in thunderstorm conditions.

Fog is essentially a cloud hugging the ground. At night, especially in the absence of cloud cover, as the land gives up the warmth that it has absorbed during the day, it may cool the air above it to the condensa-

54

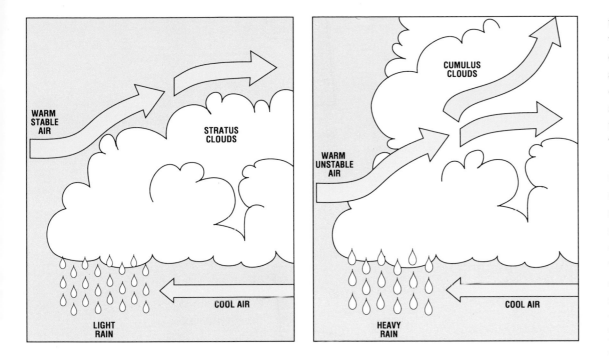

Clouds form when the warm, unstable air of a low pressure system meets and rises over the cooler air of a high pressure area. When the warm air is stable, level, or stratus, clouds form. More turbulent conditions lead to heavy rain from cumulonimbus storm clouds.

tion point. This cool air, denser than the warm air above it, hugs the ground and creeps into low-lying areas and valleys. In some areas near the ocean, fog actually contains a good percentage of the moisture absorbed by the land. Fog accounts for ten to twenty inches of moisture per month in Tasmania and Hawaii.

Perhaps the most famous fog in America is San Francisco's. Unlike ground fog, the cloud that envelops the Golden Gate Bridge and San Francisco Bay every morning is advection fog. As warm air moves over the cool surface of the Pacific Ocean, water vapor in the air condenses and forms droplets. The droplets first form at sea level, and then move higher to a level of warm air where condensation can no longer occur. Normally when clouds form, condensation occurs at higher altitudes, where the air cools the water molecules. In this case the cooling occurs closer to the surface so it is called advection.

Sky Rhymes

Reading the signs in the sky was important to early Americans who depended on the weather for shipping and farming. To make remembering cloud patterns easier, they often expressed their folklore in rhymes and verses.

Another name for the wispy cirrus clouds that tell of an approaching slow-moving warm front is mare's tails; the name for the altocumulus clouds that bring rain with a cold front is mackerel clouds.

Mare's tails, mare's tails,
Make lofty ships carry low sails.

Mackerel clouds in sky,
Expect more wet than dry.

Mare's tails

Mackerel clouds

RAIN

With clouds, of course, come rain—at least some of the time. The formation of one of nature's most basic elements—the raindrop—was a mystery until relatively recently. For raindrops to form, one ice crystal must first take shape in a supercooled cloud. Once that happens, a sort of snowball effect occurs within the cloud as the ice crystal falls, attracts supercooled water droplets, and forms more ice crystals. These in turn rise and fall again, creating even more crystals. The water molecules in the cloud are attracted to the ice crystal and as each molecule attracts others, a symmetrical pattern builds. What we feel as rain, then, starts out as a mass of swirling snowflakes within the cloud.

In order for water vapor to condense into droplets, there must be a surface of some sort on which the water can condense. Vast numbers of microscopic particles, which float in the atmosphere, can act as condensation nuclei. There are three kinds of nuclei, or centers, on which water will condense. Bits of dust, sand, or salt are called

Some studies show that rainfall levels can increase in urban areas affected by pollution. Cloud droplets form around the particles created by pollution.

ice nuclei. Cloud droplets, on the other hand, form around cloud condensation nuclei, which may be salt, smoke, or clay particles. These are smaller and more numerous than ice nuclei. Condensation nuclei are the smallest of all and are the basis for the formation of cloud condensation nuclei.

Depending on the temperature and humidity of the air, sometimes the rain won't even reach the ground. In a desert, warm air may evaporate the rain before it falls all the way. In many places, evaporation at the surface may be so rapid that rain won't have the chance to seep into the ground.

When the rains do come, they often come with force, and sometimes the results can be disastrous. Heavy rains after a drought are one such example. During January 1937, rain fell for twenty-five days straight in the midwestern United States, killing 137 people and leaving a million people homeless. In this short period of time between fourteen and nineteen inches (35 to 48cm) of rain accumulated.

Dew

Dew is the glistening film of water that beads up on blades of grass. The dew point is the temperature at which air will no longer hold water and the humidity is at 100 percent. Warm air can hold more moisture than cool air. That's why the relative humidity—the amount of water vapor in the air expressed as a percentage of the amount of water the air could hold at that temperature—is often higher on hot days. As the temperature drops, air reaches its dew point and water condenses. Dew represents cooling by radiation. Water condenses on a hard surface because the surface is cooler than the air around it. The water film that forms on a cold glass of beer on a hot day is dew.

Dew

The greater the difference between the dew point and the air temperature, the less likely it will rain. Hence the truth in the proverb:

When the dew is on the grass,
Rain will never come to pass.

Beads of dew form in the early morning on blades of grass and other structures, such as this spiderweb, low to the ground.

S N O W   A N D   H A I L

Water in its frozen state can be one of nature's most awe-inspiring phenomena. Fluffy white flakes floating gently to the ground can quickly turn into a blinding snowstorm. The mild rain shower offering relief from the summer heat may precede a deadly hailstorm. Twenty parts air to one part water, snow is a good insulator of both warmth and sound. When it accumulates on the ground, its lowest layer is the warmest as it traps the heat beneath it and reflects the sunlight hitting it from above. Eighty to ninety percent of sun's energy that falls on snow is deflected, giving it a high albedo, or ability to reflect light and heat.

When the temperature in a cloud is between 10° and -4°F (-12° and -20°C), snow may form. Ice crystals in a cloud may encounter droplets, which freeze on them, gradually building the crystals into snowflakes that float down to earth. If the temperature at the earth's surface is low enough (below 39°F or 4°C), the flakes will land; for snow to build up on the ground, the temperature must be even colder.

Hail is most likely to fall in the summertime. Hail is formed in turbulent, supercooled thunderclouds, when ice nuclei are pushed up on a warm current of air, cooled, and raised again. At heights of up to twenty-five thousand feet (7,500m), these drops freeze, and when they fall in the cool downdraft outside the warm updraft, they fall with deadly force. In 1888, hundreds of people were killed in a vicious hailstorm in India. Today, large hailstones can be equally damaging. Though scientists have experimented with ways to reduce the formation of hail in supercooled clouds, the results have been anything but conclusive.

Green and fruitful in the summertime, a Canadian farm (left) lies barren against a winter blizzard. Though the wind rages outside, snow piled up against the house helps keep it warm because snow is an excellent insulator.

Hail Brings Peace

In 1360, King Edward III of England and his army hoped to overtake Paris. When deadly hailstones began to fall from the sky, however, King Edward realized that too many of his men and horses had been killed for him to claim victory. As a result, he was forced to sign the Peace of Bretigny at the hands of nature's forces rather than those of his French enemy.

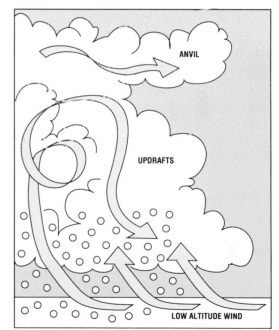

Hail forms in supercooled cumulonimbus clouds. Water droplets in the cloud grow as they rise and fall several times as a result of violent updrafts. Finally the ice crystal will fall as hail when gravity pulls it to earth.

Stormy Weather

THE IMPRESSIVE ROARING AND RUMBLING OF THE SKIES DURING A THUNDER-STORM HAS HAD GREAT IMPACT ON THE HUMAN IMAGINATION. IN NEARLY EVERY CULTURE THE FURY OF THUNDER AND LIGHTNING APPEARS IN MYTH AND LEGEND. LIGHTNING IS A PRIMARY SOURCE OF ENERGY ON EARTH. EVERY DAY, SOME TWO THOUSAND THUNDERSTORMS THAT COULD CREATE LIGHTNING OCCUR ON EARTH, AND EVERY TWENTY-FOUR HOURS, BETWEEN EIGHT AND NINE MILLION LIGHTNING BOLTS STRIKE THE GROUND. LIGHTNING MAY WELL HAVE LED TO THE "DISCOVERY" OF FIRE BY ANCIENT HUMANS. THE CUMU-LONIMBUS CLOUDS THAT PRODUCE THUNDERSTORMS ARE UNSTABLE LAYERS OF AIR FILLED WITH TREMENDOUS ENERGY. SOME ESTIMATES PUT THE POTENTIAL CHARGE BETWEEN THE TOP AND BOTTOM LAYERS OF A THUNDERCLOUD AT ONE HUNDRED MILLION VOLTS. THE AIR ROLLS WITH SOUND AND THE SKY IS LIT WITH THE ELECTRIFIED ENERGY OF LIGHTNING.

THUNDER AND LIGHTNING

The clouds that bring thunder and lightning—cumulonimbus clouds—form in the same way as other clouds, as described in Chapter Two. Cumulonimbus clouds can generate thunderstorms at any time of the year. Winter storms tend not to last as long as summer storms and produce fewer flashes of lightning. The lightning is an electrical discharge between positive and negative regions. Within cumulonimbus clouds, electrical charges build up. At the same time, the ground below the thunderclouds builds its own charge. The interaction of the two charges creates thunder and lightning.

As the cumulonimbus cloud climbs higher and higher, stretching from five thousand to forty thousand feet above the ground, the temperature difference between the top and bottom of the cloud can be as much as 100°F (37°C). The unstable air within the cloud is constantly moving, as the molecules and particles collide, which creates the positive and negative charges. The heavier particles with a negative charge collect at the bottom of the cloud, while the lighter particles, which are positively charged, rise to the top.

As the negative charges at the base of the cloud push down, electrons on the ground are forced out of the area. This creates an area of positive charge along the ground that scientists call an image or shadow. As

the old saying goes, opposites attract. This is precisely what happens with the image on the ground and the negative charges at the base of the cloud. As the cloud moves along with the winds, the image is pulled along beneath it. Air, like ceramic and plastic, is a good insulator so the negative charge of the cloud and the positive charge of the ground don't meet. However, the area beneath the cloud may lose its insulation if the negative charges are strong enough to attract the nuclei of the atoms in the air and push away the electrons. The air in this state is called plasma, which is an excellent conductor of electricity.

Now the negative charges in the cloud and the image on the ground intensify their attempts to meet. The cloud forms a leader of negative charges flowing down. Meanwhile, the positively charged image tries to reach up to the leader and will climb to any heights to reach it, creating its own leader. That's why high buildings and trees are likely to be hit by lightning. The image flows up these objects as it reaches for the negatively charged leader that is simultaneously reaching down for the image. In fact, the cloud sends down many leaders, one extending from the next in a series of short bursts. (This creates the sometimes forked or jagged appearance of lightning bolts.) About one hundred feet above the ground, the image and cloud leaders meet and the image sends a charge up this newly created

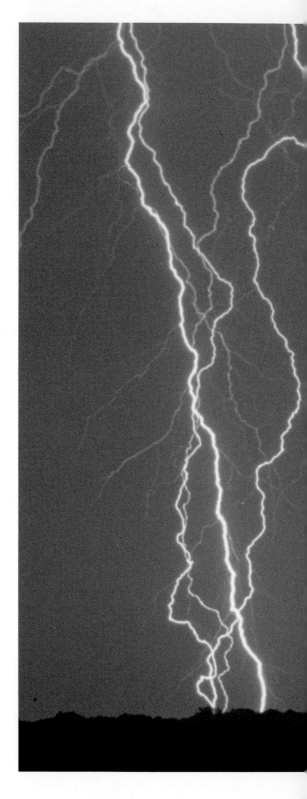

Lightning strokes can occur singly or together, depending on the paths of conductivity opened between the charged cloud and the ground. Bolts that appear crooked are actually a series of many lead strokes.

tunnel. This is called the return stroke and is what we actually see when a lightning bolt hits the ground.

While physicists generally agree that thunderclouds are filled with electrical energy that leads to a lightning bolt, they still don't fully understand how the process works. Recent lightning research shows that lighting is more powerful and faster than previously thought. Estimates now say that the power of a lightning bolt can be four hundred thousand amps per millionth of a second, some twenty times faster than scientists previously believed. To arrive at these results, scientists launched three-foot-long rockets, which were tied to the ground by a

Lightning occurs in a cumulonimbus storm cloud when a tunnel of negative charges, known as a "leader," flows toward the ground from the cloud. From the ground, a positively charged leader pushes toward it and the two meet about 100 feet (30m) above the surface. At this point, the charge from the ground runs up into the cloud. This is known as the "return stroke" and is what we see when lightning bolts light the sky.

Gods of Thunder and Lightning

THOR.

Thor, the Norse god of thunder.

Thunderstorms are such a powerful force in our world that ancient civilizations attributed them to the power of the gods. In southwestern Native American lore, lightning is a snake traveling from heaven to earth. Other Native Americans believed that the flash of lightning was the flapping of the thunderbird's wings. Damage from lightning was, of course, caused by the bird's claws.

In Greek myth, Prometheus was the fire bringer. He stole fire from the gods and brought it to earth for humans to use. Perhaps this myth tells the story of how humans first harnessed fire from a blaze set by a stroke of lightning.

Thunder was a powerful force to be reckoned with, too. In Teutonic mythology, Thor, the god of thunder, was among the most powerful of gods. The sound of thunder was Thor's chariot rolling across the sky. With his mighty hammer he would strike down his enemies and was regarded as a skillful and powerful warrior.

Lei-kung, the Chinese god of thunder, was just as powerful. He often used his chisels to punish those who had committed crimes against the gods or to chase out evil spirits.

Shelter from the Storm

Lightning presents such a threat to human beings and their belongings that many amazing methods have been developed in attempts to avoid it. During the Middle Ages, popular theory held that ringing cathedral bells would stop lightning from hitting the church. The phrase *Fulgura Frango*, "I break up the lightning," was often cast in the bells, but it didn't hold true. The practice ended after many bell ringers were killed. In the Ozark Mountains, on the other hand, legend has it that hiding scissors will prevent lightning from striking.

Short of putting a lightning rod atop our homes, we know that we can do little to calm these savage storms. More picnics than can be remembered have been interrupted by a sudden, violent summer thunderstorm. Out there in the rain and wind, it's natural to want to seek shelter, but when lightning is involved, you're better off lying flat in a field if you can't make it to your car. The best thing to do is follow the accepted safety procedures:

* Remain in your car, or
* Lie down flat in a field, and
* Never attempt to take shelter under a tree.

wire, into electrified clouds. The rockets upset the electrical charges in the cloud and created a lightning bolt that traveled down the wire. The research was conducted to study how to reduce the danger to the space shuttle and other spacecraft. The results lead researchers to believe that nearly three quarters of the spacecraft hit by lightning created the charge that hit them. Scientists have yet to determine exactly how to identify which clouds will produce an electrical charge when a rocket or spacecraft is launched into them.

The flashes of light we sometimes see in clouds that never reach the ground are called sheet, or heat, lightning and are generated by the same process that creates the bolts that do hit the ground. Sheet lightning occurs when a cloud is so charged that lightning is produced within the cloud itself.

When lightning does hit the ground, it can be extremely destructive. Lightning sparks forest fires, rips bark off trees, and, when it hits power lines and other good electricity conductors, can cause power blackouts. The researchers who studied lightning and spacecraft believe that the protective distribution arrestors on power lines are not fast enough to stop the surge of an electrical charge from lightning. Lightning is so powerful that many hapless picnickers and golfers have been electrocuted by its power. In the United States, a full 15 percent of deaths caused by lightning occur because people seek protection under a tree. A lone tree in a field is the worst place to be in a storm. As we saw, the image will seek the path of least resistance to the negative charges in the cloud, which makes tall objects the most likely candidates for being struck by lightning.

When lightning hits a tree, the bark actually explodes off it. The water in the tree is a good electricity conductor. As the lightning travels through the tree to the ground, the bark is heated, and the tree's water creates steam that heats so quickly it literally pushes the bark off the tree. Sometimes lightning will start a fire. On July 12, 1940, 335 forest fires were started as lightning struck the western United States. Estimates indicate that two-thirds of all forest fires start as a result of lightning.

Benjamin Franklin devised the single most common protective device against lightning. A pioneer in the study of electricity, Franklin published an article in *Poor Richard's Almanac* in 1753 showing how to install a controversial new invention, the lightning rod. When affixed to the top of a building, the lightning rod creates a cone of protection around the building. James Trefil explains how a lightning rod works: "The iron lightning rod represents a sort of superhighway [to the lightning]. The house is also a possible conducting path but resembles an overgrown and rocky logging road. Given the choice, the current takes the superhighway every time."

Thunder is the sound created when the air around the lightning's return stroke is heated and expands. The heated air pushes at the still air around it at supersonic speed, creating first a shock wave, then a sound wave. All of this happens in less than a second. Thunder is produced at different points along the stroke, which results in a rolling or booming sound rather than just one big bang. The wave from the pocket of air around the stroke heated first reaches us first, those farther away a little later. Another factor influencing the sound we hear is our position in relation to the thunder. Thunder produced within a few hundred yards of one person will sound different to someone half a mile away.

Lightning Strikes Twice

If you've heard that lightning never strikes twice in the same place, think again. Because the charged particles on the ground and in the cloud are trying to reach each other, electricity will take the path of least resistance, which usually means the tallest object around. This means that tall buildings and trees may offer repeat lightning performances. The Empire State Building in New York City, for example, has been hit many times since it was first built.

How Far Away Is It?

Count the number of seconds between the flash of lightning and the sound of thunder and divide by five. This will tell you how far away the lightning is in thousands of feet because sound travels one thousand feet per second.

In China, where the monsoons dump huge amounts of rain in a short period of time, water buffalo plow the fertile fields.

When the Rain Doesn't Pour

Monsoons are probably the only floods in the world that are welcome. Everywhere else, floods mean damage to crops and buildings and cost lives. In areas where the monsoons occur every year, people have learned to live around the floods they bring. In fact, they worship them. Disaster strikes when the monsoon fails—as the drought of 1877 tragically showed. Thousands of people died, and it provided the impetus for long-range weather forecasting.

MONSOONS

As the Arabic origin of its name indicates, monsoons (from *mausim,* meaning season) are seasonal rains that arrive every spring in eastern India, Vietnam, and the northern Philippines. A week after the rains begin, widespread flooding occurs. Though they cause flooding, the monsoons are necessary for the survival of the area's agriculture. The monsoons do not cause the damage and loss of life heavy rains do in other parts of the world. The people here have adapted their lives to the monsoons. One town in the Brahmaputra valley in Assam receives an average 424 inches (1060cm) of rain every summer.

The rains come when the winds shift as the temperature rises over the land in summer. During the winter when the land cools, the winds flow from land to sea. During the summer, the wind blows from the sea, bringing the much-needed rain.

When the monsoons fail, crops also fail and widespread starvation can occur.

Throughout history, the monsoons have failed many times and scientists believe their failure has led to the downfall of at least one ancient civilization. Along the Indus River, archaeologists have discovered artifacts of a five-thousand-year-old civilization called the Harappans. While we still can't read their writing and know very little about them, climatologist Reid Bryson believes the Harappans perished when the rains failed. Between 3,600 and 10,000 years ago, the rains that fell in Sambhar Lake, their major source of water, were much greater. When the monsoons didn't come, the lake dried up and the ensuing drought lasted for seven hundred years. 2,900 years ago, the lake filled again. Although theirs was a heavily agricultural economy, the Harappans hadn't developed irrigation, which spelled death for them when the monsoons failed. At one time the Harappan empire covered a quarter million miles of modern India and Pakistan that today is desert.

STORM SURGES AND BOMBS

T hough a storm in the Bay of Bengal cost one million lives in 1970, normally those areas that can expect the monsoons are prepared for the tremendous flooding that coincides with them. The amount of rain that the monsoons dump in these areas has quite a different effect than violent rains in areas unused to the steady downpours. Storm surges, which create a sudden rise in the sea level because a low pressure system "piles up" water in front of itself as it approaches

Storms gather power as they kick up more energy from the water as they travel across the ocean. When they hit land, their power dissipates, but coastal areas suffer high winds and saturation as waves crash into shore at incredible heights.

Whether a tropical storm or hurricane, or a winter storm along the northern Atlantic coast, no sea wall can keep out the fury of an ocean tossed by the effects of a storm.

the coast, have cost many lives and millions of dollars in damage. In 1953, 494 miles (790km) of land normally protected from the surging sea by a series of dikes was flooded in Holland when a low pressure storm system surged in from the north. That storm claimed 1,800 lives and caused weeks of flooding, resulting in huge property losses. In the same year, another storm surged down the North Sea across Scotland and Northern Ireland capsizing a ferryboat and killing 307 people in all.

In an attempt to better predict the direction and intensity of North Atlantic low-pressure storms that affect the eastern seaboard of North America, the United States Navy and meteorologists have begun the Experiment on Rapidly Intensifying Cyclones (ERICA). The six-million-dollar ERICA research grew out of a 1986 study called GALE (Genesis of Atlantic Lows Experiment), which studied how storms form off the mid-Atlantic coast. These storms form when cool air from the north and warm air from the tropics collide. The GALE research shows, however, that the Appalachian Mountains and Gulf Stream have more influence on these storms than meteorologists had thought.

Using buoys, reports from planes, and other instruments, the meteorologists involved with ERICA hope to learn even more about the activity of these storms at sea. They'd like to know why some storms, which appear to be mild winter storms, suddenly become "bombs" as they move north and hit New York and Cape Cod with snow, ice, and high winds. After the scientists have analyzed the results of their 1988–1989 study, they may be able to help predict which storms will become bombs.

TORNADOES

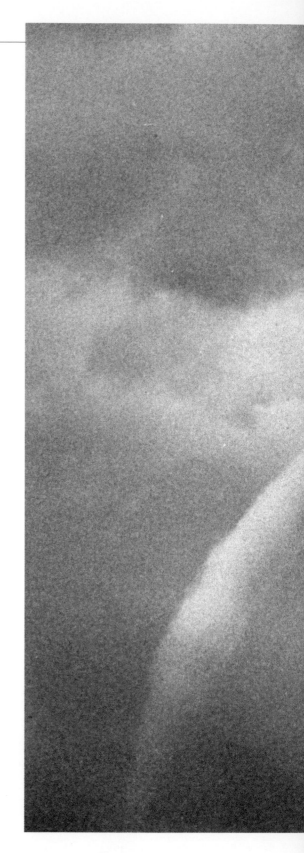

The world's most famous tornado hit Kansas and whisked Dorothy and Toto off to the Land of Oz. If only the aftermath of real-life tornadoes could be as sweet. The twisters that wreak havoc on the Great Plains of America every year from the spring through the early fall don't bring to mind the yellow brick road to most people who experience them. For all the random destruction they leave in their paths, a tornado has also been known to lift a baby from her cradle and deposit her safely in a garden down the block. With winds as high as 224 miles (358km) per hour, the average seven hundred tornadoes that strike the United States every year more often than not flatten everything in their narrow paths.

In the Great Plains region, a tornado forms when cold, dry air from the Rockies blows in over warm air from the south. As we know, warm air rises, which makes the air in this situation very unstable. If the day is very warm, or if a cold front moves in, the air will rise violently and create storms. Tornadoes often are preceded by thunderstorms and lightning, and the sky frequently glows with an eerie green cast. They begin as funnel clouds, which reach down from a cloud toward the ground. As with a hurricane, a tornado's center is an area of intense low pressure. Around the center, the air spins in a counterclockwise direction. The spinning starts when a strong updraft of very warm (and often very moist) air lasts for a few minutes and the air around it moves in, producing the funnel.

Tornadoes usually travel at about twenty-five miles (40km) per hour, and some have reached speeds of sixty-two miles (100km) per hour. The average life of a tornado is twenty to thirty minutes, although some have lasted up to several hours. While tornadoes generally travel toward the northeast, it is less easy to predict where the funnel will touch ground. The erratic tornado may rip through one town and bounce over the next, leaving it unharmed. In one case, a tornado left the ground but was low enough to lift the tops off a row of buildings. Another intriguing aspect of the tornado's path of destruction is that sometimes the storm is narrow enough to destroy one side of a street while causing only minor wind damage to the houses on the other side.

A tornado's intense low pressure is perhaps more deadly than the strong winds that accompany it. The difference in pressure between buildings and the outside air causes the structures to actually explode. As happened with Dorothy's house in Kansas, the whirling winds of tornadoes often are strong enough to pick up even heavy objects and carry them for several miles. Sometimes, as with the baby, they seem to be put gently back down on earth. Scientists believe this occurs when there is enough updraft to cushion the object's fall.

Tornadoes claim more than one hundred lives per year in North America and cause millions of dollars in damage to crops and buildings. The only safe place to be in these violent twisters is a storm cellar. While storm-watch systems do alert the public to the possibility of a tornado hitting an area, the storms generally are too unpredictable for weather services to forecast their paths accurately.

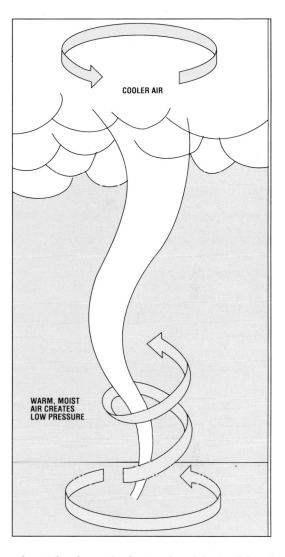

COOLER AIR

WARM, MOIST
AIR CREATES
LOW PRESSURE

Above: Though tornadoes begin as funnel clouds, all funnel clouds will not become tornadoes. For a tornado to form, hot, moist air at the surface rises and meets cold, dry air above it; air rushes in at the ground level and the spin of the tornado begins. The vortex of the tornado reaches high inside the cloud from which it forms.

Though narrow, the swirling vortex of a tornado destroys everything in its path when it touches ground. Seeing one coming is terrifying enough, but the sound can be just as frightening. "Tornado" derives from the Spanish word for thunder. To some the tornado sounds like a fleet of jet aircraft, to others like a train speeding through a tunnel. Still others have described the sound as "the bellowing of a million mad bulls."

As this view from above shows, the counterclockwise swirl of a hurricane draws moisture and energy into its powerful vortex as it feeds itself on the tropical ocean.

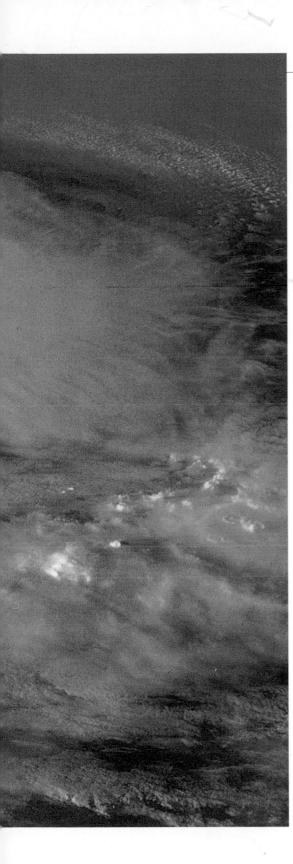

HURRICANES

The fierce winds of hurricanes sweep across all of the world's oceans except the South Atlantic. They strike primarily the northwestern Pacific, the Bay of Bengal, the southwestern Indian Ocean, and the oceans north of Australia. Called typhoons in China (from _tai fung_, meaning wind which strikes) or in some places tropical cyclones, these storms are whirling low pressure systems that by some estimates are powered by more energy than some nuclear weapons. (The heat-energy release in hurricane clouds alone has been estimated to be about one thousand times the amount of electric power generated in the United States.) Hurricanes are distinguished from the low pressure systems from which they spring by the force of their winds and their counterclockwise motion. The genesis of a hurricane is a tropical disturbance, which has no strong winds and no cyclonic movement. Its big sister, the tropical depression, brings winds of up to thirty-eight miles (60km) per hour. The next step, the tropical storm, is the true parent of the hurricane and lashes the land with winds of up to sixty-nine miles (110km) per hour.

The hurricane may whip the wind toward its center at up to 112 miles (180km) per hour, and can stretch for 375 miles (600km). By hurricane standards, a storm of this size is relatively mild. At the hurricane's center is the eye, an area of low pressure that can measure from almost four to twenty-five miles (40km) across. The larger the eye, the calmer the winds. One particularly bad storm in 1979, typhoon Tip, brought winds of up to 190 miles (300km) per hour, was fourteen hundred miles (2,240km) in diameter, and possessed the lowest pressure of any hurricane on record.

The hurricanes that threaten southeastern and eastern North America travel across the ocean with the trade winds. As they move, the low pressure at the center of the storm is fed by condensation from the warm waters beneath it. As warm air is pulled into the low pressure area at the core of the hurricane, it rises and condenses to form clouds, which are pushed away from the center of the storm. The heat that is generated with the formation of cloud droplets warms the storm's center, causing even more warm air to be drawn into the storm to rise and form more clouds. As the hurricane gains momentum, it greedily feeds itself on the sea spray it kicks up as the winds increase. High waves add to the area of contact between water and air and intensify the transfer of water and heat from the ocean to the atmosphere.

Hurricanes only form in warm, moist conditions in the tropics between five degrees and twenty degrees north and south of the equator. The water temperature must be at least 80°F (27°C). However, hurricanes generally do not form within five degrees of the equator. Here the Coriolis effect, which gives the hurricane its distinctive spin, is negligible. When a low pressure system develops in this region, the air around it moves in to balance the pressure.

Under the influence of the Coriolis effect, the counterclockwise-swirling vortex of a storm takes shape when a low pressure area

forms because the air surrounding the low pressure area is pushed away. The Coriolis effect and westerly winds move the hurricane along between ten and twenty miles (16 and 32km) per hour, gradually moving it away from the equator. At the Caribbean, it turns north where it is affected by the Northern Hemisphere's upper-westerly winds and where the cooler water temperatures make the hurricane's movement and force unpredictable. When the storm meets land it loses steam, no longer fed by the waves or the high winds of the sea. If it meets a warm low

pressure area, it may revive, pushing heavy rains northeast across the Atlantic as far as Britain.

Even so, hurricanes do hit land with tremendous force, bringing high winds that push waves to unbelievable heights. Winds can be so strong initially that they can "drive a plank of wood right through the trunk of a palm tree and blow straws end-on through sheets of corrugated iron." The eye of the storm, which at sea was the storm's calm, moist center, warmer than the storm around it and oppressively humid,

eventually dies. Land doesn't have the warm moisture necessary to feed the storm so the winds calm a bit and heavy rains begin. The rains increase because there is greater friction with the ground, which causes more air to rise, forming more rain clouds.

The rains, and resulting floods and landslides, can be even more damaging than the high winds of the hurricane. The island of Baquio in the Philippines was entirely covered with three feet of water because of one storm. In 1896, Mauritius in the Indian Ocean

*Unlike human structures, the palm tree is perfectly adapt-
ed to tropical storms, which are characterized by high
winds. Palm trees bend with the wind and survive where
stiff structures are destroyed.*

*As beautiful as the Florida coast may be, humans too often
underestimate the power of tropical storms and hurricanes.*

received no less than forty-seven inches
(117cm) of rain in four days. Another hurricane dumped almost two feet (60cm) of
water in one day on Texas in 1921. While
these are astounding figures, measuring the
rain from a hurricane can be a difficult task.
Winds moving at more than fifty-six miles
(90km) per hour drive the rain horizontally,
making standard rain-gauge readings inaccu-
rate. On average, a hurricane of average size
and force will dump between three and six
inches (7 and 16cm) of rain.

Hurricanes can change the face of an
entire island. They can destroy crops and
flatten trees and buildings. In tropical areas
that often experience hurricanes, vegetation
and trees have adapted to the fury of the
wind. The palm tree, for example, will bend
with the wind and will likely remain stand-
ing, while human shelters are devastated.

Raging Ladies

Before the 1940s, hurricanes weren't
identified by human names. Legend
has it that lexicographer George
Stewart's novel *Storm*, published in 1941,
started the trend because the meteorologists
in the book named their storms. Perhaps
under the influence of this meteorological lit-
erary legend, World War II meteorologists
began to name hurricanes. The United States
Weather Bureau instituted an alphabetized
system in 1953 and began to alternate male
with female names in 1979.

Other accounts say that an Australian,
Clement Wragge, began the practice during
the early twentieth century by naming hurricanes after people he liked.

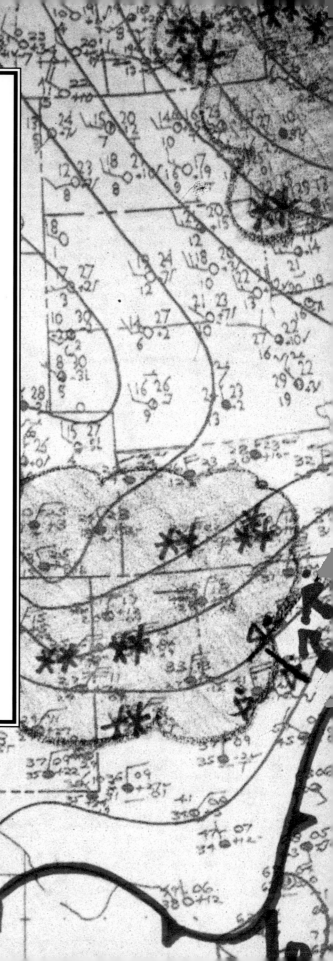

Weather Forecasting

Some are weatherwise, some are otherwise...
—Benjamin Franklin

GIVEN THE NUMBER OF GODS AND MYTHS ASSOCIATED WITH WEATHER PHE-
NOMENA, HUMANS SEEM TO HAVE BEEN AVID WEATHER WATCHERS FROM THE
VERY BEGINNING. ANCIENT CIVILIZATIONS RECOGNIZED THE IMPORTANCE OF
PREDICTING THE SEASONS IN ORDER TO HUNT FOR AND PRODUCE FOOD, AND
THEY DEVISED COMPLEX SYSTEMS TO PREDICT THE WEATHER BASED ON THE
STARS AND PLANETS. TODAY, OUR PREDICTIONS ARE BASED ON MORE TECHNO-
LOGICALLY SOUND EVIDENCE, BUT THE BASIC INGREDIENT OF WEATHER PRE-
DICTION IS STILL OBSERVATION, WHETHER THROUGH ANALYSIS OF UPPER AIR
CONDITIONS WITH WEATHER BALLOONS AND SATELLITES OR WITH THE NAKED
EYE AND AN INTUITIVE SENSE OF THE ENVIRONMENT. IRONICALLY, THE MOST
SOPHISTICATED OF OUR WEATHER-WATCHING TECHNIQUES CAME NOT FROM
THE NEED TO FEED OURSELVES, BUT FROM WAR: THE NEEDS OF WAR HISTORI-
CALLY HAVE PROVIDED THE IMPETUS TO DEVELOP MORE RELIABLE METHODS OF
WEATHER PREDICTION.

Weather-watching records as we know them today have been kept for only the past one hundred to two hundred years. Yet in humanity's short history on earth, we have kept records nearly as long as we have tilled the soil for food and observed the behavior of animals on the hunt. Still, accurate predictions for the day-to-day weather are comparatively new. In fact, the term "forecast" wasn't used consistently in weather reporting until 1889. Before then, meteorologists discussed weather "probabilities" or "indications."

The first written weather observations come from ancient Babylon in the seventh century B.C. Omens such as the movement of stars and planets, a meteor falling to earth, and the appearance of solar and lunar halos formed the basis of these early records. In ancient Egypt, the calendar was developed by observing cycles of the stars and sun and matching those to weather patterns. Astronomer-priests noted a fourteen-year cycle of flooding of the Nile, which was crucial to Egyptian agriculture. Three-thousand-year-old records from China show that the early Chinese also matched seasonal weather patterns with planetary movements.

The Greeks and Romans also relied on astrology, an influence that persisted through to the seventeenth century. For two thousand years, the magnum opus of meteorology was Aristotle's (384–322 B.C.) *Meteorologica*. Though Greek mythology attributed weather to the whims of the gods (as in the Homeric epics The *Iliad* and The *Odyssey*), Aristotle applied some "scientific" observations of planetary movements to come up with his encyclopedia of weather patterns. The Roman writers Pliny and Ptolemy also relied on astrology to explain the weather and drew heavily on Aristotle's work.

While Aristotle's *Meteorologica* recorded observable phenomena, it attempted no weather predictions. The first almanacs, called *prognostica*, were published during the medieval period. Based on astrological events, these often attempted specific predictions for a particular day, and, though several disastrous floods and freezing periods were falsely predicted, they were still quite popular. During the sixteenth century some three thousand *prognostica* were published by six hundred different prognosticators.

During the Middle Ages, Aristotelian meteorology had become so influential that it was adopted as church doctrine. Alongside their astronomical tables and almanacs, scientists noted weather events. Between the thirteenth and seventeenth centuries, the records show a shift away from the astronomy to observation of the weather events themselves. The efforts of astronomers and scientists, like Nicolaus Copernicus (1473–1543), who proposed that the earth revolved around the sun, were often repudiated by the authorities of the day. It was not until the philosophical revolution of the seventeenth and eighteenth centuries that scientific attempts to evaluate weather phenomena fell on more receptive ears.

Finally, scientists began to concentrate on meteorological phenomena rather than on astronomy. Evangelista Torricelli invented the first thermometer in 1643 and Robert Boyle invented the barometer in 1665. By the close of the seventeenth century, mercury barometers were widely available. The hydrometer, which measures humidity, was also invented during this period.

When early meteorologists began to record basic weather data, predicting weather patterns was still very unsophisticated. Almanacs, the descendants of

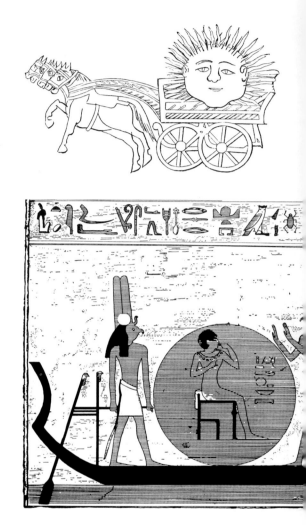

Though ancient civilizations recorded the movements of celestial phenomena like the sun, noting their correspondence to crops and the seasons, they created powerful images and myths to explain their existence. In an old Persian manuscript, the sun rides across the sky in a chariot. In an Egyptian scene, the sun journeys across the country on a boat.

Medieval knowledge of the weather depended on Aristotle's observations in Meteorologica. *Nicolaus Copernicus (above) challenged the scientific status quo when he presented his heliocentric theory. Copernicus's work radicalized our understanding of the heavens, which in turn contributed to our modern understanding of weather patterns.*

prognostica, were popular weather predictors for farmers during the eighteenth and nineteenth centuries. "Almanac" derives from the Arabic word for "calendar of the skies," and almanacs of the time still relied heavily on astronomical and superstitious notions of celestial phenomena. Even Benjamin Franklin, the great inventor and scientist, included superstitious sayings in the tremendously popular *Poor Richard's Almanac,* published annually between 1732 and 1757. (During its peak years, Franklin's almanac sold as many as ten thousand copies.)

The early weather forecasters realized that only the collation of data from different parts of the globe would offer a comprehensive view of weather patterns. The first such effort was sponsored by Grand Duke Ferdinand II of Tuscany in 1653. Edmund Halley, the scientist who charted the course of Halley's Comet, was the first to offer a map of the earth's wind patterns. Later, based on The Royal Society of London's weather figures gathered from all over Europe (a project that began in 1723), George Hadley noted varying areas of pressure around the world, which led to his theory of global convection cells. Starting with twelve stations in 1780, the Mannheim Meteorological Society quickly expanded to fifty stations in 1781 and pioneered the use of weather symbols, some of which are still used today.

Synoptic weather maps, which display conditions over a wide geographic area and are used to predict the weather, were developed in Europe during the early nineteenth century. However, it was impossible to quickly compile all the data at a central location because communication was slow and cumbersome. With the invention of the telegraph and Morse Code in 1832, meteorologists had a much faster way to collect the data. Benjamin Franklin is credited with doing the first synoptic weather study when he tracked a storm's movement from Georgia to Boston in 1743. When the Smithsonian Institution began compiling data from two hundred observers across the United States in 1849, we began to understand weather patterns in North America.

While Native Americans had some sense of these weather patterns, the new settlers had to build up their own knowledge of their new land's weather over time. The first accounts were, of course, limited to the East Coast. Captain John Smith published *A Description of New England* in 1616, which was followed in 1634 by William Wood's description of New England's weather, *New England Prospects*. Wood's work was propagandistic in tone and designed to lure settlers to the region. The first "weatherman" in America was Reverend John Campanius Holm, who kept daily records of the weather along the Delaware River from the time he settled in America in 1643.

Benjamin Franklin's famous key-with-kite experiment led to his invention of the lightning rod. Franklin showed that lightning was a form of electricity. He also liked to watch the weather and published his predictions in Poor Richard's Almanac *during the mid-eighteenth century.*

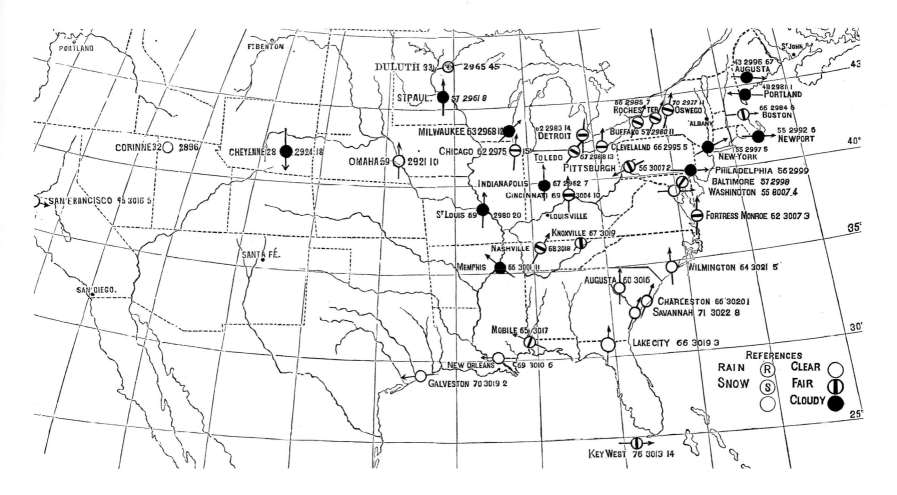

Early weather maps, this one dated 1871, showed the temperature, barometric presure, and force of the wind in a given city.

B y 1857, with the westward expansion of the United States and the use of the Smithsonian Institution's weather watchers, enough information was available for the "father of American climatology," Lorin Blodget, to publish *Climatology of the United States and the Temperate Latitudes of the North American Continent.* The public first enjoyed the results of weather-watching when the *Washington Evening Post* in America and the *Daily News* in England published daily tables of weather statistics in 1848.

The Civil War brought a temporary halt to the work of meteorologists in the United States, but in Europe, war led to the expansion of the weather-watching network. After the Anglo-French fleet was destroyed in a storm during the Crimean War, the British military began issuing three-day storm forecasts in 1861 to avoid another such catastrophe. The French meteorologist Le Verrier began publishing daily reports in 1863 from the Paris Observatory. He introduced isobars, which note pressure systems on weather maps.

After the Civil War, the Federal Meteorological Service was founded in 1870. In 1890, it was reorganized under a civilian organization, the United States Weather Bureau. By 1908, the Weather Bureau published its first weekly predictions.

THE MODERN FORECAST

During the early twentieth century, meteorologist Vilhelm Bjerknes proposed that the two requirements for predicting the weather were to observe the weather locally and to understand what caused the various effects and how "one state of the atmosphere develops from another." During World War I, he and his son Jacob coined the term front, visualizing the masses of air that create the weather as troops on a battlefield. Bjerknes understood that by identifying fronts all over the world he could show widespread weather patterns and relieve meteorology of some of its more subjective methods of prediction.

The Bergen Geophysical Institute was founded by Bjerknes in 1917, when World War I cut off Norway from the rest of Europe—making a Norwegian weather forecasting system necessary. Tor Bergerson of the Bergen School contributed another important element in modern weather-forecasting when he classified air masses by their thermal properties and moisture content.

In Britain, Lewis F. Richardson was trying to predict the weather with mathematical formulas, but performing the equations manually was slow and unwieldy. By World War II, the technology was available to develop computers sophisticated enough to handle these kinds of mathematical operations. The development of computers sped up with the increasing wartime needs for decoding secret codes and for forecasting the weather for military operations. The early computer prototype, ENIAC (Electronic Numerical Integrator And Computer), was born during this period and carried over into peacetime use due to the efforts of John Von Neumann at Princeton. He and Jules Charney came up with more streamlined equations to successfully forecast the weather.

Finally, using satellites in space and computers complex enough to analyze the data, weather predictors could meet the two requirements set forth by Bjerknes for forecasting the weather. During the 1960s, global weather watching evolved with the formation of the World Meteorological Organization (WMO) and the International Council of Scientific Unions (ICSU). Then-president of the United States, John F. Kennedy, proposed a worldwide effort to understand the weather that led to the formation of the World Weather Watch (WWW) in 1968. With 150 member nations, the WWW analyzes weather data from 9,200 land stations and 7,000 ships. Eight hundred-fifty of those stations report on upper-air conditions and five geostationary and five polar-orbiting satellites provide a global view of weather conditions. Readings at the stations are taken at 00, 06, 12, and 18 hours Greenwich mean time (upper-air soundings at 00 and 12 GMT, wind-finding flights at 06 and 18 GMT) and distributed to three world centers located in Washington, Moscow, and Melbourne. These world-wide centers in turn distribute the data to twenty-one regional centers, which are responsible for passing the information along to national centers.

In the United States, a complex system of computers compiles the daily weather maps used to disseminate weather informa-

Though they seem crude to us now, the instruments early weather-watchers used really aren't so different from our modern equipment. Top, the watchers take readings from a wind gauge, barometer, and hygrometer. Though our tools are more sophisticated, one method hasn't changed much since the nineteenth century—visual reports.

tion to the public and to agencies like the Federal Aviation Administration. The National Oceanic and Atmospheric Association's (NOAA) Cyber 205 supercomputers process vast amounts of numerical data from satellites and other weather-observers. Then, the 9000-series computers translate the information into a format that is usable by humans.

The main computer at the National Meteorological Center in Camp Springs, Maryland, the Cyber 205A, creates a computerized "twin earth" that analyzes what's happening in the atmosphere by dividing it into many layers of boxes, each about the size of Kansas. The supercomputer is fed eighty billion bits of information from weather stations and satellites every day, which is processed through a series of five equations (the basic laws of physics) to predict, ten minutes at a time, what the weather will do. The computer needs one hour to complete a three-day forecast and goes through some 150 billion arithmetic operations in all.

Using these supercomputers, meteorologists have been able to double the forecast period. Even so, determining the accuracy of a forecast is difficult, at best. If the forecast calls for cloudy skies, cool temperatures, and chance of rain, can we say the forecast is accurate if the skies clear by mid-afternoon and the temperature remains cool? Generally, however, the computers are at their best for one-day predictions, and three-day forecasts are moderately accurate. The computer has predicted wind-flow around the earth for a six-day period, but these forecasts have not proved very useful in predicting an area's weather because they are too general.

The twin-earth computerized image is known as a General Circulation Model. To predict the day-to-day weather, the Cyber 205 will need to be refined, showing more boxes with finer resolution. Air can be unpredictable, and, as meteorologist Edward Lorenz of the Massachusetts Institute of Technology suggests, "the flap of a butterfly's wings in Brazil can start a tornado in Texas."

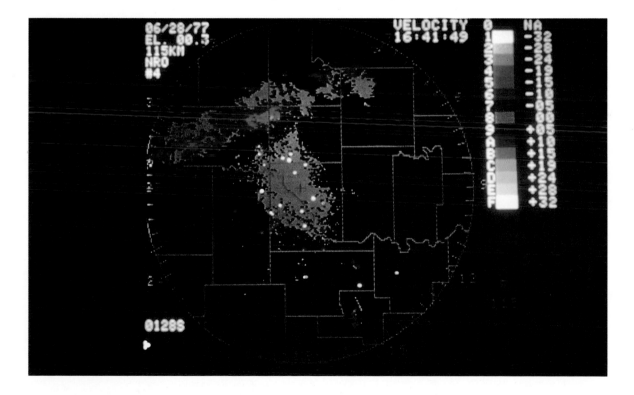

Unlike traditional radar, which picks up only the presence of an object, Doppler radar analyzes echoes to show the direction and speed of a storm. The system is effective for tracking severe storms (as shown here) and for studying a relatively new weather phenomenon, micro- and macrobursts. The small and isolated bursts, a kind of wind shear, were responsible for the famous crash of Delta 191 in Dallas in 1985. Cold, dense air in a thundercloud rushes downward. Delta 191 entered the undetected microburst just after the air hit the ground and spiralled up, creating 60-mile-per hour tail winds for the jet. Unable to recover, it crashed, killing 133 and injuring 31.

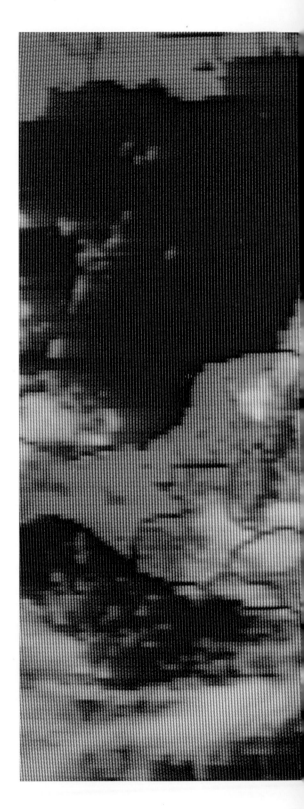

BALLOONS AND SATELLITES

The computers that process the weather data are fed by a massive system of weather-monitoring stations and satellites. Information from radio-sonde balloons provides readings of the upper atmosphere's humidity and temperature while ground stations, boats, and planes report on conditions closer to the surface.

As high as twenty-two thousand miles (35,000km) above the earth, satellites monitor the movement of the jet streams and the activity of the weather all around the world. Some satellites orbit the globe in twenty-four hours, keeping up with the rotation of the earth so that they appear to remain in one spot over the earth. These are the geostationary satellites. Other satellites, called polar orbiters, circle the globe from pole to pole and give us a picture of the whole planet.

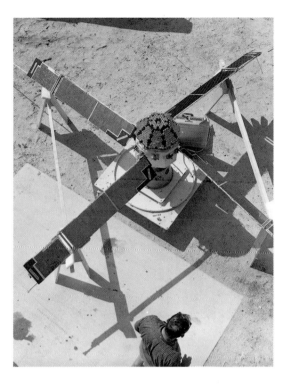

The first weather satellite—TIROS, Television and Infra-Red Observation Satellite—was launched in 1960. Other satellites, like this 1964 Beacon Explorer, measure ionosphere electron densities in their polar orbits. Currently, the National Oceanic and Atmospheric Administration relies on polar-orbiting and geostationary satellites to collect weather data.

Satellite pictures help meteorologists track major storms. Though storm-trackers can successfully predict the direction and speed of a hurricane, changes in temperature and wind speeds sometimes surprise them. Hurricane Gilbert ripped across Mexico in 1988, missing the coast of Texas where weather-watchers predicted it would hit.

Skylights

No ATMOSPHERIC PHENOMENA HAVE FASCINATED HUMANS QUITE AS MUCH AS COLORFUL HALOS AND RAINBOWS. EVEN TODAY, AN OBSERVER MIGHT ATTRIBUTE TO A COLORFUL SUNSET OR TIMELY RAINBOW SOME SPIRITUAL OR MYSTICAL SIGNIFICANCE. YET WE NORMALLY EXPLAIN THESE PHENOMENA SCI-ENTIFICALLY. TRADITIONALLY, OUR MECHANISTIC, NEWTONIAN WORLD VIEW EXPLAINED RAINBOWS AND OTHER PHENOMENA IN TERMS OF A FIXED SET OF PARTICLES IN THE ATMOSPHERE WHOSE REFLECTIVENESS COULD BE EXPLAINED MATHEMATICALLY. TODAY, PHYSICS EMBRACES THE IDEA THAT ALL OBJECTS AND PHENOMENA ARE MERELY WAVES OF ENERGY. BEGINNING WITH AN UNDERSTANDING OF NEWTONIAN CLASSICAL OPTICS AND MOVING TOWARD OUR MODERN UNDERSTANDING OF WAVE THEORY AND PARTICLE PHYSICS, WE CAN SEE HOW COLORS IN THE SKY REALLY ARE MYSTICAL—EVEN FROM A SCI-ENTIFIC POINT OF VIEW. PHYSICS EXPLAINS ATMOSPHERIC PHENOMENA THROUGH UNDERSTANDING HOW LIGHT WAVES MOVE AND HOW LIGHT TRAV-ELING THROUGH ATOMS AND PARTICLES IN THE ATMOSPHERE WILL BEHAVE.

Like sound, light travels in a series of electromagnetic waves. Each color in the color spectrum is a different length: the longest waves are at the red end of the spectrum while the shortest waves are blue and violet. A light wave from which no waves have been filtered is white and contains all colors. When a light wave hits a particle in the atmosphere, the particle changes the direction the wave travels. Part of the wave enters the particle and is refracted, while some of it bounces away from the particle and is reflected. The colors we see are produced by the particles through which the light passes. This is why we can tell the quality and content of the air by observing the colors in the sky (see "Visibility," page 93). The colors we see also depend on the angle at which we observe these light waves being reflected and refracted as they collide with particles in the atmosphere.

The laws of reflection and refraction explain the basics of many optical phenomena. *Reflected* light bounces off a particle at the same angle it hits it. *Refracted* light bends because the material it passes through changes its path, sending the light wave in a different direction. Refraction makes the sun appear higher in the sky than it actually is because the light waves are bent before reaching our eyes. This principle makes a person's legs appear shorter than they are when they stand in a pool. Sunlight is reflected off the surface of the water, while the light entering the water is refracted. The person's legs appear shorter because the light is refracted by the water. In the same way, the sun's light is refracted by the atmosphere.

NOTE: When looking at the sky for any of the phenomena discussed in this chapter, never look directly at the sun.

Green Flash

The infrequently sighted green flash has suffered from the skepticism of scientists. When conditions are just right, a brilliant green flash may appear atop the sun before it sinks below the horizon. Scientists interested in atmospheric optical phenomena had, until the mid-twentieth century, dismissed this unusual sight as fantasy.

Weakening the credibility of the green flash was its history in non-scientific publications. In fact, popular interest in the flash began not with an article in a scientific journal, but with a science fiction novel by Jules Verne published in 1882, *Le Rayon Vert*. Also, because it is seen so seldom, the flash was explained away by the fallibility of the human eye. Some argued that

because looking at the bright light of the sun causes eye fatigue, the flash was simply a figment of the viewer's imagination. It could be merely that the eye saw red's complement on the color wheel, green. The same effect occurs when we look at a bright light. If we turn our eyes away quickly, we see another color.

Despite this skepticism, scientists have

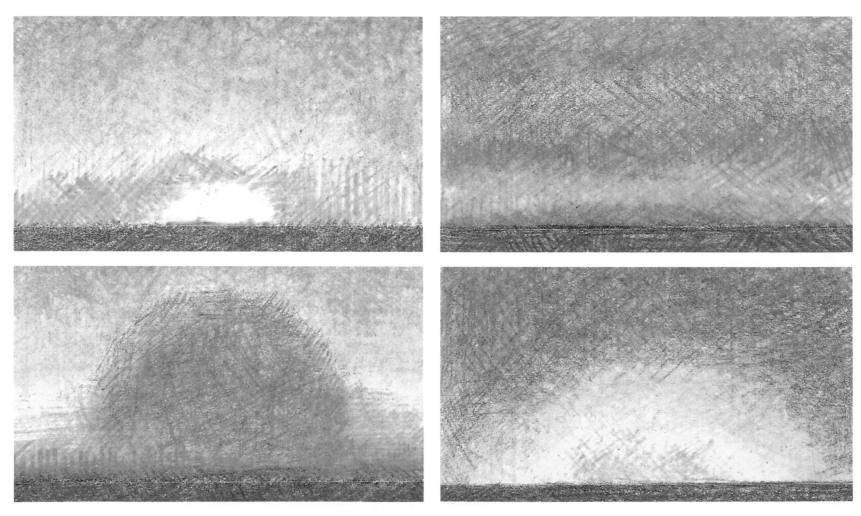

now accepted the existence of the green flash and come up with an explanation for it. When the sun hits the particles in the atmosphere, the blue end of the light spectrum is scattered, which makes the sky blue. As the sun sets, the light waves must travel through more of the atmosphere and blue gradually is winnowed out. This is why the sky often takes on a reddish hue at sunset. At dawn and dusk, light waves are dispersed most because the sun is at its greatest angle to the observer and light waves travel through more of the atmosphere. Red light has the longest wavelength, and as the sun sinks, we see the red light of the sunset disappear first, then orange, yellow, green, blue, and violet. Some observers have reported seeing blue or violet flashes, though these are uncommon because they are so short. Observers report seeing them most often at high elevations.

To see this uncommon green light, there must be a clear sky. The more particles in the air, the more light is absorbed, making the chance of seeing the green flash even less likely. A good pair of binoculars or a telescope pointed at the sun just before it sinks may help you to see the flash. Chances are best at high altitudes, in tropical seas, and in deserts.

As the sun sets towards the horizon, light waves pass through the atmosphere at different angles. This creates the various colors of the sunset. As the last waves of light enter the atmosphere, a green flash may appear (lower right).

Visibility

The atmosphere naturally contains an unimaginable number of submicroscopic dust particles from soil, smoke, salt from ocean spray, bacteria, seeds and spores, volcanic ash, and meteoric dust. Hundreds of these particles can be found in just one cubic centimeter of air. Visibility reflects the number of particles in the air. When visibility is good, the atmosphere is stable; when visibility is poor, there are more particles in the air. Variations in the concentrations of these particles can create blue, gray, or even brown haze.

Blue haze is often seen in the Smoky Mountains of the American southeast. While blue haze does not decrease visibility, it does add a smoky blue hue to everything it covers and casts a unique blue light on distant objects. Scientists aren't sure exactly what causes this kind of haze, but their guess is that it is created when terpenes (a type of hydrocarbon found in some kinds of vegetation) and ozone particles mix.

Gray haze is composed of larger bits of soil, salt, and minerals and occurs most often in the spring when pollen and spores fill the air. Gray haze obscures visibility and resembles the brown and smoky blue haze produced by human pollution.

Brown haze, commonly known as smog or pollution, can hang in the air over an area and severely limit visibility. Haze of this sort has been known to reach as high as three miles (4.8km) into the atmosphere.

Dust particles in the air, whether produced from human waste or naturally, add texture to the sunlight streaming through the atmosphere to earth. Water molecules are attracted to some of these particles and form the droplets that make clouds. When the air is full of particles and the sun is hidden, crepuscular sun rays can be seen. These are beams of sunlight streaming down through the clouds spread out in a fan shape.

Blue Ridge Mountains

Covenant of the Rainbow

To many cultures, the rainbow is a sign that the stormy seas of suffering have come to an end. In the Judeo-Christian tradition, the rainbow was a sign from God to Noah that a flood would never again destroy the earth. According to the book of Genesis (9: 12-16), God said, "I set my bow in the cloud, and it shall be a sign of the covenant between me and the earth. When I bring clouds over the earth and the bow is seen in the clouds, I will remember my covenant which is between me and you and every living creature of all flesh; and the waters shall never again become a flood to destroy all flesh."

THE RAINBOW

Whether it is interpreted as a sign that suffering will come to an end or seen as a path to a pot of gold for some lucky leprechaun, the rainbow is, as African mythology tells us, the servant of thunder, a gloriously peaceful spectrum of color often seen in the sky after a rainstorm.

Rainbows are formed when the sun illuminates water droplets in the sky. Scientists have long sought to explain exactly what occurs to form the elusive rainbow. Aristotle correctly theorized that a rainbow is simply light reflected at a fixed angle, yet he believed the reflected light came from a whole cloud rather than separate water droplets. Based on the work of the German monk Theodoric of Freiberg, the French philosopher and mathematician René Descartes (1596–1650) laid the groundwork for explaining the rainbow mathematically. In 1304, Freiberg hypothesized that each water droplet in a cloud could create its

own rainbow as light was reflected once from each droplet's inner surface. Descartes realized that for a rainbow to appear, the light must be reflected at a particular angle in a water droplet, which he explained mathematically by geometrical optics. Both Descartes and Theodoric knew that the colors of the rainbow each came from a different set of water droplets. While Descartes showed how a ray of light would behave when it hit a water droplet at a number of different angles, and that the brightness of a rainbow depends on the angles of the rays, he couldn't explain how or why a rainbow was composed of different colors.

In 1666, Sir Isaac Newton showed that light is really a combination of different colors, or wavelengths. Newton's prism experiments showed that for each wavelength, or color, the refractive index differs. (The refractive index is a measure of the speed at which light passes through a substance.) In

other words, we can think of a rainbow as a series of rainbows side by side, ranging from violet on its inner edge through the spectrum to blue, green, yellow, orange, and red on the outer edge.

Sometimes, a secondary rainbow, produced when light is reflected twice inside the water droplet, appears next to the first, or primary bow. The secondary rainbow's colors appears in reverse order. The dark area of the sky between the two rainbows is known as Alexander's dark band.

While Descartes and Newton explained the basic rainbow, their calculations could not account for Alexander's dark band or supernumerary arcs. Supernumerary arcs are bands of pink and green light that sometimes appear on the inner, violet edge of the primary rainbow. In 1803, Thomas Young dispelled the mystery of these colorful arcs by showing that the same light rays that produce the rainbow can interfere with each other given a particular droplet size

Left: Rainbows occur whenever water droplets in the sky catch light rays at the right angle. At sunrise and sunset a half-bow like this one sometimes appears.

Right: The colors in a secondary rainbow are fainter and occur in reverse order from the primary rainbow. A secondary rainbow occurs in water droplets above the primary bow when light is reflected twice inside the droplets, reducing the energy of the light rays.

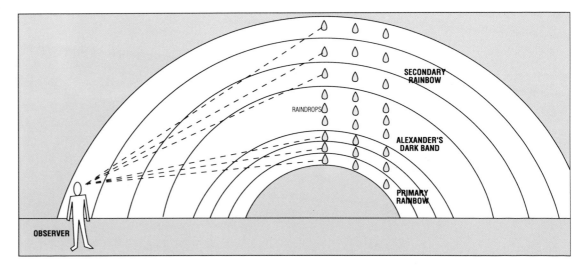

and scattering angle. The smaller the droplet, the greater the angle at which the light rays interfere, thus the greater the chance of supernumerary arcs. Because water droplets tend to increase in size as they fall, supernumerary arcs are most often seen near the top of a rainbow. Occasionally, a portion of the arc may appear to be missing—this means either that no rain is falling in that place (hence, no water droplets) or that the droplets are not illuminated by the sun, perhaps because the shadow of a cloud obstructs it.

To fully explain these phenomena, scientists examine the behavior, or physics, of the light itself. Light moves in waves just as sound does. Alexander's dark band can also be explained by understanding how light waves move. George B. Airy contributed an important equation to understanding rainbows by determining the distribution and intensity of light with new mathematical formulas. Known as the Airy function, it shows that the maximum rainbow angle is a little greater than the minimum scattering angle computed by Descartes.

Still, even though mathematicians and scientists could now understand the rainbow in mathematical terms, physicists had yet to explain the real mechanics of the bright belts in the sky. In other words, we can understand the rainbow mathematically, but we don't understand what it is exactly that we are describing mathematically. Physicists think of the rainbow in terms of electromagnetic waves, and look at what happens to an electromagnetic wave when it is scattered by water droplets into a series of partial waves to define a rainbow. Explaining these partial waves mathematically involves many complex calculations. As a sort of shortcut, G.N. Watson came up with the complex-angular-momentum theory. This says that a photon, which has energy but no mass, is reflected several times within a water droplet. The theory explains the rainbow in terms of a few mathematically manageable points, rather than a series of complicated terms.

Morning or late in the afternoon are the best times to see rainbows, because when the sun is high in the sky, the tops of rainbows are low and more difficult to see. When we see a bright, vibrant rainbow, the water droplets in the sky are large. Smaller droplets create a rainbow with duller colors that overlap.

THE GLORY

Imagine flying in a plane at thirty thousand feet. Looking out the window, you see the shadow of your plane against the clouds. Suddenly you notice the shadow is surrounded by a rainbow of color. What you're witnessing is called the glory, or pilot's bow. It may well be called the "glory" because of its appearance in religious iconography from Greek, Roman, and Christian paintings and sculpture to Chinese and Indian depictions. In their 1974 article in *Scientific American*, Howard C. Bryant and Nelson Jarmie speculate that pictures of the glory around the heads of religious figures "could have arisen from the observation of such halos on fog banks by solitary mystics on well-illuminated heights."

Of all the skylights, this is the only one in which the observer's own shadow plays a role in creating the effect. The glory always appears when the observer is between the sun and uniform water droplets. The glory appears around the shadow cast on the cloud of droplets.

The glory occurs when light from water droplets in the cloud is scattered back toward the sun, which enhances the scattering of the light. Light is scattered from the edge of the droplets and the light rays are reflected at a specific angle within them.

Scientists use wave optics to explain the glory. When the highs and lows of a wave meet, they are in phase. When the highs and lows don't meet, they are out of phase. Scientists use the term *interference* to explain when the waves are in or out of phase. Interference simply means that when two waves meet, they will enhance or diminish each other. When waves interfere constructively, they are in phase. Destructive interference describes waves that are out of phase. In their laboratory experiments, scientists have found that the glory is brighter when the water droplets are bigger because the reflected light rays interfere constructively.

HALOS

As with the glory, halos inspire mystic and religious wonder. Halos often appear as colorful circles around the sun, but they also may form crosses in the sky or give the appearance of a "double sun." As one writer describes it: "Halos stir one's mind and soul, since they probe both the physical environment of the cloud and one's awareness and appreciation of the natural world." In fact, because they form when ice crystals are in the air, halos may often warn of bad weather approaching. As we know, cirrus clouds often precede low pressure storm areas. These cirrus clouds contain the ice crystals that create halos.

Particle theory tells us that rainbows and the glory result from the reflection and refraction of light by water molecules. Halos form in much the same way except that ice crystals, not molecules, create the mysterious glow around the sun. Ice crystals can take many shapes, at least four of which are responsible for atmospheric halos: the plate, column, capped column, and bullet crystal. These four types of crystals possess the sixty- and ninety-degree angles within their forms that are necessary to create a halo when light strikes them.

Brownian motion says that ice crystals randomly move through the air because of their collisions with molecules in the air and that if the crystals are large enough and all of the same type, they will line up, or orient themselves, in the same way. The most common halo, the twenty-two-

A foggy Everglades sunrise.

degree halo, is formed by randomly oriented crystals. (The degree refers to the angle at which the light from the halo reaches the observer.) While the twenty-two-degree halo is the most common, halos can be anywhere from eight to thirty-two degrees.

The deviation of light in the crystals explains the appearance of the halo. Deviation is the angle between the incident ray and the ray leaving the crystal. Imagine a ray of light entering and then taking a turn inside a crystal. The angle at which it takes that turn is the deviation. For a halo to appear, the minimum deviation (a principle of classical optics) must occur. Light accumulates at the minimum deviation angle.

Halos sometimes look like circular rainbows because the minimum deviation depends on the angle between the faces of the ice crystals and the refractive index. As we saw, the refractive index for each wavelength of light is different, producing a different color. Dispersion creates the differently colored rings. The reddish halos are smaller than the others and appear on the inner edge.

Sometimes halos appear with "parhelia" (from the Greek for with the sun), which are spots of light on or outside the halo. Also known as sun dogs and mock suns, they are brighter than the halo. When the sun is low in the sky, sometimes a bluish white tail will appear.

Other halo phenomena you may see around the sun include the rare; brightly colored circumzenith arc, the circumhorizon arc, Parry arcs, and the parhelic circle and solar pillar. The parhelic circle, solar pillar, and twenty-two-degree halo sometimes appear together, forming a cross in the sky.

The sun dog, surrounding a halo, appears brighter than the halo, ringed with blue and white light.

_F_rightful Lights

Native tribes living in the far north who witnessed the spectacular aurora borealis regarded the nighttime displays with wonder and a little fear. They believed that the aurora was the result of dueling and angry gods carrying torches across the sky. In the Hudson Bay area, Inuit peoples attributed the aurora borealis to evil spirits looking for lost souls. Farther south, where the aurora is seldom seen, it had an even more frightening effect in 1585. That year, the aurora borealis was seen by French peasants who, thinking the sky was on fire and that their end was near, flocked to their churches to pray.

If aurorae appear on a given night, they show up at about midnight and may change in shape and intensity throughout the display.

AURORAS

While the atmospheric phenomena we've discussed so far all result from the interplay of light with particles in the atmosphere, the auroras display lights in the sky far above the earth's surface in the ionosphere. Scientists see a correlation between the appearance of the auroras (borealis in the Northern Hemisphere, australis in the Southern Hemisphere) and the activity of solar flares. The sun's stream of particles occasionally intensifies, shooting more ions at earth (see Chapter Two). The earth's magnetic field deflects these ions except at the poles, where they move directly into the ionosphere. Here, they create the spectacular streaks of light of the auroras, also known as the "northern and southern dawn."

Auroras are most often seen in a circle twenty-three degrees from the magnetic poles. The general range for seeing the auroras is between 60 and 45 degrees of latitude. Though the latest intense solar flare in March 1989 led to sightings by amateur observers in upstate New York, it is almost never seen below 45 degrees. (In 1958, a solar flare was so intense that the aurora was seen as far south as Redmond, Oregon; Vermillion, South Dakota; Williams Bay, Wisconsin; Ithaca, New York; and Hanover, New Hampshire.) The best place to view the aurora borealis is around the southern part of Hudson Bay in Canada. Interestingly enough, sightings decrease as you move northward.

The region where the aurora is visible is known as the oval zone. Any activity of particles in the ionosphere here will produce a polar-cap glow. For example, after a particularly powerful solar flare, the oval zone will be cast in a whitish green. After high-altitude nuclear bomb tests, the area has been bathed in a crimson color. The size of the oval fluctuates with the intensity of the sun's activity. When the sun's activity is low, the oval shrinks towards the geomagnetic poles; when the sun's activity is high, it grows.

Auroras are green, pink, and red, and sometimes show violet and blue light. The colors reflect the makeup of the particles in the upper atmosphere. When the light is green and red, excited oxygen atoms are present. Violet and blue light indicate the presence of ionized nitrogen. Weak red light probably means that hydrogen atoms are in the area.

Most auroras begin around midnight and progress from a faint glow on the horizon or a patch of light to ribbons of light to cloudlike patches or coronae in the sky. The ribbons appear stacked one on top of the next and can take four forms. The smooth homogeneous arc is the calmest of the four and is brightest at its lowest point. The rayed arc appears when the electrons in the atmosphere become more active, and individual rays appear. Curtainlike folds may also appear in the ribbons of color, creating a rayed band. The rayed band can evolve into a type B aurora if the atoms in the atmosphere continue to be excited. Now a pink glow will appear at the bottom of the ribbon. The rarest, and most active of all auroras, is called type A. These appear a rosy color with a whitish green band.

Some auroral displays are quiet, keeping to a single form all night, while others change, surging and moving across the sky. The faintest displays are colorless or may appear pale green; the most striking aurorae may be bright red or show yellow or blue tinges.

BALL LIGHTNING AND ST. ELMO'S FIRE

Much mystery surrounds these two phenomena. While scientists have yet to fully explain them, it is believed that they do truly exist and are not merely the result of the imaginations of amateur observers.

Ball lightning in particular garners much skepticism. Science has yet to explain why this phenomenon occurs and several theories have been proposed over the years. Ball lightning most often appears after a lightning stroke and can be anywhere from six inches to one foot in diameter. The ball may remain in the sky for a few minutes (though a few seconds is more common)

and will travel along power lines and other conductive paths. Some observers report that a ball will enter an open window, travel around the room and then leave. In London, one man reported that ball lightning leapt into a barrel filled with four gallons of water, which then boiled for a few minutes. If this account is true, then ball lightning must be full of energy, yet damage from it has been slight, sometimes scorching wood and burning through wires. While it does pack a punch, it doesn't appear to be as powerful as a lightning bolt.

If indeed ball lightning does exist, scientists have yet to conclusively prove how it

The legend of St. Elmo's Fire originated with sailors. They saw the mysterious burst of light at the top of their masts as a sign of protection from God. Ironically, the appearance of St. Elmo's Fire may mean that conditions are right for lightning to strike.

forms and how it keeps glowing. One line of reasoning maintains that ball lightning is singly ionized, which means that the atoms or molecules in the air are minus one electron. When these particles recombine, they produce the heat and light of ball lightning. However, molecules in this state are very unstable and the recombination and neutralization required to create the ball of lightning would take less than a second, not long enough to sustain ball lightning. How does the ball last for as long as it does if it is formed of this plasma of electrons and ions?

Two theories seek to explain ball lightning: One says that energy is fed into the ball from the outside while the other maintains that the ball is formed with enough energy in it to keep itself going. Russian physicist Peter Kapitza theorized in 1955 that ball lightning maintains itself from energy created by the lightning bolt from which it formed in the first place. According to his theory, electromagnetic waves absorb the ionized energy from the lightning where it collects in troughs. Thus the ball lightning would continually feed itself. However, scientists do not believe that lightning possesses the kinds of electromagnetic waves crucial to Kaptiza's theory. Another problem with Kapitza's theory is the story of ball lightning boiling water. If this story is true, how did the ball continue to generate energy while cut off from its source in the water?

Another theory maintains that the ball lightning somehow feeds on its own energy. As physicist James Trefil explains it in *Meditations at Sunset*, "the ball is actually a species of miniature thundercloud. The original stroke somehow produces oppositely charged regions from bits of material, such as dust motes, that are normally in the air.

The millions of tiny lightning strokes that neutralize these charges are what is seen as the glow of the ball lightning. Although this scheme explains how a ball could live a relatively long time, it gives no explanation of why a lightning bolt should produce a neatly segregated set of charged particles in the first place."

While ball lightning eludes scientists, it hasn't earned the same prophetic significance as St. Elmo's Fire. St. Elmo is the patron saint of sailors; this "fire" is named after an Italian bishop who lived around A.D. 300. By most accounts, the association of St. Elmo's Fire with safe travel on the sea originated with the voyage of Ferdinand Magellan during the sixteenth century. Reportedly, the ship was being tossed about by a storm and the sailors feared they were about to meet their maker when one of them saw St. Elmo's Fire. After that, the storm ceased and the sailors saw it as a sign that no harm would come to them.

However, the electrical charges that produce St. Elmo's Fire can be quite dangerous: The conditions that lead to St. Elmo's Fire are close to those that produce a lightning storm. Seen atop ships' masts, flagpoles, church steeples, and around airplane propellers, the green (and sometimes blue) light of the "fire" is produced when a large positive charge flows up an object to get to an electrically charged cloud. The air around the object is ionized and some electrons are pulled toward the object. As the electrons are pulled, the air heats up, causing the greenish glow.

Between 1810 and 1815 some fifty-eight ships were struck by St. Elmo's Fire. Mountain climbers have reported seeing the glow around their ice axes and Swiss peasants say the horns of cattle in high pastures may glow, creating "flaming horns."

Weather Cycles

Without its many protective layers of atmosphere, earth could not sustain life. The atmosphere exchanges water and other molecules with the earth, thereby creating the weather and the basis for life. The atmosphere also acts as a sort of porous blanket, keeping the surface warm by trapping and distributing its heat and screening out harmful ultraviolet rays from the sun. This characteristic of the atmosphere is known as the greenhouse effect and is of great concern to scientists and citizens alike.

In the stratosphere, the ozone layer acts as earth's insulator. It allows light and heat from the sun to reach earth while screening out harmful ultraviolet rays. As the earth and oceans warm, heat radiates skyward and is trapped by the ozone layer, helping earth maintain its moderate global climate. The primary greenhouse gases—carbon dioxide, methane, and nitrous oxide—trap most of the earth's heat.

Earth often has been described as a self-regulating system, exchanging water, oxygen, carbon dioxide, and other elements between the atmosphere and the land and oceans. When one element is depleted or increases, the system will compensate for that change. Scientists now believe that the increase in the greenhouse gases, along with the growing holes in the ozone layer at the poles, leave earth poised on the brink of a dramatic global climate change. Yet it remains to be seen exactly how earth will compensate for the higher levels of greenhouse gases. As we saw in Chapter One, the weather is affected by not only the simple exchange of energy and water from earth to sky, but also by the placement of the continents, earth's magnetism, fluctuations in radiation from the sun, and the position and tilt of earth in space. Scientists also have yet to calculate in the effects of possible added cloud cover, how the oceans will respond, and other factors.

There are many pieces in earth's climate puzzle. The closer scientists get to putting them together, the more we realize that there are serious ramifications to human interaction with the environment. As we know, some climate change occurs with or without human influence on the atmosphere, but many scientists believe that our actions have set an unprecedented change in motion. Only time will tell if climate change will occur gradually over hundreds of years or suddenly in the space of a decade or two. Only time will tell if we can use the same technology that has endangered earth and humans to implement remedies for the negative effects we've set in motion.

The burning of fossil fuels and the emission of other wastes into the atmosphere upset the delicate balance of gases in the atmosphere. Three gases in the atmosphere before the Industrial Revolution—methane, carbon dioxide, and nitrous oxide—have increased 1 percent, 0.4 percent, and 0.2 percent annually. Other gases such as Fluorocarbon 12 and Fluorocarbon 11, with 20,000 and 17,500 times the ability of carbon dioxide to trap heat, are distinctly human contributions to the greenhouse gases. They currently increase in the atmosphere at a rate of 5 percent per year.

GREENHOUSE GASES

Of the greenhouse gases, carbon dioxide causes environmentalists and scientists the most concern. Humans now produce much of the carbon dioxide in the atmosphere through the burning of fossil fuels, and to a slightly lesser, but still significant, extent, the burning of forests. Carbon dioxide has earned a bad name in the past couple of years but when it occurs naturally, it is one of the principal elements necessary to sustain life. In photosynthesis, plants absorb carbon dioxide and release two atoms of oxygen for each broken down carbon dioxide molecule. In the atmosphere, carbon dioxide acts as an excellent insulator, letting in visible light from the sun and reradiating infrared energy from the surface back to earth. In this way, the atmosphere acts like greenhouse glass, which also lets in sunlight, but lets little of its heat escape. As Jonathan Weiner, author of *Planet Earth*, points out, comparing the atmosphere to greenhouse glass is something of a misnomer since "a greenhouse holds in warmth because the glass keeps hot air from rising and blowing away. Carbon dioxide is part of the air itself and holds in warmth because it keeps *radiation* from getting away."

While carbon dioxide and methane have served as earth's insulators almost since the atmosphere was first formed, their role has changed from a beneficent one for humans to one that could become quite threatening in our lifetime. In fact, a number of scientists believe we are already experiencing the effects of an increase in the greenhouse effect.

Studies of carbon dioxide levels in the atmosphere show that before the industrial revolution of the mid-nineteenth century, levels of carbon dioxide were considerably lower than they are now. Deforestation, automobile emissions, and other fossil-fuel burners have literally pumped up the carbon dioxide level, disrupting the delicate balance of the atmosphere and making the greenhouse effect a danger to rather than a guardian of the earth's temperate global climate.

In 1958, Charles David Keeling of the Scripps Institution of Oceanography began to study carbon dioxide levels in the atmosphere of Hawaii. His findings showed that at that time there were 315 parts per million of carbon dioxide in the atmosphere. Every year since then, the level of carbon dioxide has increased by as much as one-and-a-half parts per million. Given the increased production of carbon dioxide in the last two decades (about 500 million tons every year), the amount of carbon dioxide may double by the year 2040 to about 600 parts per million.

Scientists note that the amount of carbon dioxide in atmosphere changes from spring to fall. Researchers believe the levels are lower in the fall because plants have absorbed much of it during the summer. In the spring, the carbon dioxide levels have risen because humans and animals continued to produce carbon dioxide all winter while the plants were at rest.

In the spring of 1988, Dr. James E. Hansen of the Goddard Institute for Space Studies testified before a Senate subcommittee that we are indeed experiencing the effects of this increase in carbon dioxide in the atmosphere. Based on studies of carbon dioxide, scientists postulated some of the potential results of the greenhouse effect during the early 1970s, yet they (and the public) were reluctant to conclude that it posed any imminent danger. The extraordinarily warm temperatures of the 1980s, however, led Dr. Hansen to bring the greenhouse effect out of the theoretical realm to the forefront of public concern and policy. Some may argue that this warm trend may represent normal fluctuations in the earth's temperatures, but many agree that we could be witnessing the first sparks of a global fire.

PREDICTING THE HEAT

Today, almost everyone agrees that global warming is inevitable, but scientists can't be sure how much or for how long. Because of this, predicting the consequences is a guessing game at best. One reason for the uncertainty is our lack of real knowledge about the changes in earth's climate throughout history. We do know that earth has warmed and cooled many times, but we can only guess what brought about some of the dramatic changes in earth's profile, such as the extinction of the dinosaurs 65 million years ago. We think the climate then was much warmer than it is now; could their demise have been caused by changes in climate? Were those changes gradual or did they occur rapidly, within a few years? Dr. Wallace S. Broecker, of Columbia University, says that some data show that between ten thousand and thirteen thousand years ago, the climate changed dramatically and quickly.

To show how the earth's atmosphere and climate might respond to changes in the amount of carbon dioxide in the atmosphere, scientists use supercomputers to recreate earth's climate at various points in history and to predict how it might change with an increase in greenhouse gases. These global circulation models (see Chapter Five) offer a tantalizing array of variables, but no conclusive results as yet. For example, using the computer at the National Center for Atmospheric Research, Eric Barron tried to show how the earth could have reached the high temperatures of the Cretaceous period 100 million years ago. Scientists believe that during this period the earth was warm even at the poles and that overall temperatures were 43° to 54°F (6° to 12°C) higher than they are now. In his model, Barron recreated the location of the continents, computed the probable wind patterns, and waited for the earth to heat up. While the model heated the earth to one-third of what we think temperatures were at the time, it let the oceans evaporate, which filled the atmosphere with water vapor and formed a cloud cover so dense that the earth cooled. Even so, Barron's experiments did show that more carbon dioxide in the atmosphere would warm the earth.

Some data shows that in the past one hundred years, the global temperature has risen by 1°F. Estimates show that the earth will heat up another 3.5°F by 2040; other predictions say that the earth may be as much as 8°F warmer by the mid-twenty-first century. Still other studies show that global warming may range from a little over 6°F to over 11°F. Walter Orr Roberts of the University Corporation for Atmospheric Research says that the temperature at the poles could increase by as much as 18°F, melting the polar ice caps and flooding coastal areas.

Ocean temperatures may be among the primary indicators of the imminence of the greenhouse effect. Some believe that temperature readings of the ocean surface from satellites provide a more accurate measure of earth's climate change than land-based readings. Scientists say this is because urban areas are naturally warmer than normal. NOAA satellites measured ocean surface temperatures from some three million different points, and compared them to fifty thousand sea-level points from ships and buoys between 1982 and 1988. The results show that ocean temperatures had risen more than 1°F, a tremendous increase in a short period of time. While satellite readings can be distorted by dust and ash in the atmosphere, comparing them with sea-level readings gives scientists a truer picture of the actual average temperature. Scientists caution that other decades exhibit similar temperature fluctuations—for example, the 1930s were warmer than normal and the 1960s were cooler—and that ten years offers less than a fraction of a dot on the time line of earth's history. On the other hand, these findings do support the theory of global warming.

One of the results of changes in global weather patterns may be drought in areas accustomed to ample rainfall and flooding in areas used to moderate precipitation.

CONSEQUENCES

If the earth does heat up dramatically, the ramifications will be felt the world over. Sea levels, which already are rising at a rate of one-and-a-half millimeters per year, might rise even further with the breakup of ice in the Antarctic. The ice caps have a tremendous influence on wind patterns. If the winds change, weather patterns all over the globe will be affected. Wet, fertile areas could experience drought, and dry areas could be flooded by unusual amounts of rainfall. If the ice breaks up suddenly, sea levels could rise sixteen to twenty feet (5 to 6m) and cause major flooding.

It's quite likely that the West Antarctic ice cap could break up quickly. Most of the West Antarctic ice shelf extends out over the water. Unlike the East Antarctic ice, these shelves are delicate and can change quickly because they are not fixed to rock. Scientists believe the East Antarctic ice sheet did melt once over two or three centuries. Sudden melting of this massive chunk of ice could raise the sea level two hundred feet (60m).

These ice sheets are of concern to scientists particularly because of the recent discovery of ice streams, which are ten to fifteen miles wide. These flow between huge crevasses toward the sea. Scientists don't yet know how these will react to global warming, and studying their movement may tell them something about how the ice caps will react to higher temperatures. What puzzles them most at present is why one part of the ice is moving toward the sea while the other ice remains stationary. It could be that because the bottom layer of ice is warmest, the ice there melts and creates the flows. Scientists also theorize that the flows originate where ice meets rock.

Global warming also would affect world wind patterns. As explained in Chapter Three, the variations in temperature and the warm air moving from the tropics toward the poles create the wind patterns as we know them. As Walter Orr Roberts of the University Corporation for Atmospheric Research told Jonathan Weiner in *Planet Earth*, the changing wind patterns may make "the dust bowl of the 30s... seem like children's play in comparison with the dust bowl of the 2040s.... The soils will desiccate, and the winds will lift them to the skies."

Changes like these, in addition to the dangers already imposed by our increased exposure to ultraviolet rays, could lead to severe health problems. Stephen Schneider of the National Center for Atmospheric Research (NCAR) points out that some diseases now isolated in the tropics—malaria, schistosomiasis, and elephantiasis—might spread to colder climates because parasites could thrive in the warmer conditions.

FEEDBACKS

Predictions for the world's overall warming vary because of the fallibility of the global circulation models, one of the primary theoretical research tools scientists use to study the greenhouse effect. The global models are limited because they take into account only a few of the many variables that comprise the earth's environment. Atmospheric conditions not factored into the models include clouds and the effects of ocean-atmosphere exchange. In addition, scientists can only guess at such variables as the introduction of gases from vegetation and pollution from humans into the atmosphere. The interaction of these many variables in earth's environment is known as feedback. Like a thermostat on a refrigerator, a feedback is a self-regulating mechanism that changes the rate or magnitude of a process. Scientists just aren't sure how the oceans, cloud cover, and deforestation and pollution will affect the earth's warming trend.

The oceans currently absorb about half the carbon dioxide emitted by humans, which it circulates from the surface to its depths. As water heats, it loses its ability to retain carbon dioxide. Scientists wonder how quickly the oceans will be able to circulate carbon dioxide (and its heat) from the surface to the ocean floor as the earth warms. With dramatic changes in ocean temperatures, scientists also expect that ocean currents, which play a significant role in our weather patterns, will change. Scientists don't know exactly when or how the ocean currents will be affected. Computer models tell researchers only about the upper layer of the ocean and can't predict horizontal currents or probable salinity levels in the water.

The presence of water vapor and clouds in a warming atmosphere presents perhaps the most unpredictable variable in evaluating the greenhouse effect. Water vapor holds more heat than any greenhouse gas. As the atmosphere warms, the humidity and cloud cover will increase. Cloud cover might reduce the amount of warmth reaching earth from the sun. Some estimates suggest that if clouds blocked just one percent of the sun, the warming trend would cool. Another cloud-cover variable is the precipitation it would produce. If it comes in the form of snow, the planet would cool even more. Others argue that clouds trap tremendous amounts of heat and would exacerbate the warming trend.

Methane, another of the greenhouse gases, presents yet another feedback variable. Pressure in the oceans will increase as they warm. This will release methane hydrate (or methane ice) from mud under the sea floor. Other sources of methane include wetlands and rice paddies, where plants decay under water, and waste from cattle. A more surprising methane source is the termite. Some estimates say that there are some 200 quadrillion termites alive for every person on earth. Termites emit an estimated 100 million tons of methane per year: That's between one-quarter and one-half of all the methane in the atmosphere. Studies conducted in the Guatemalan rain forest, Kenya, and elsewhere around the world show that the amount of methane in

Volcanic eruptions, like Mt. St. Helens, spew tons of ash and gases into the atmosphere. Volcanoes represent one of many unpredictable feedbacks that make predicting weather changes difficult.

Swidden, or slash-and-burn deforestation, destroys precious rain forest. The rain forest plays an important role in earth's climate because it absorbs huge amounts of carbon dioxide. Burning rain forests creates great clouds of smoke that pollute the atmosphere with carbon dioxide and leaves a barren landscape ripe for rapid population by termites, which produce methane.

the atmosphere has doubled in the last 150 years and continues to increase some two percent every year.

Aggravating the termite problem is the rapid and widespread destruction of tropical rain forests. Third World countries employ a form of agriculture known as *swidden*. In Africa, South America, and Asia, many acres of forest are burned every year to make more land available for farming. As more forest is destroyed (enough to cover the state of Connecticut each year), the termite population rises, thus producing more methane. Scientists most fear that the rain forests soon won't be able to absorb enough carbon dioxide to keep the climate's temperate balance. Smoke from burning the forest emits even more carbon dioxide into the air.

The role vegetation plays in absorbing carbon dioxide also is an unpredictable feedback. Scientists don't know if increased carbon dioxide levels will cause plants to decay more quickly, or if the plants will adapt to the rising levels by absorbing even more carbon dioxide. Studies of bristlecone pine trees in Arizona show that the trees thrive on carbon dioxide, which, as Jonathan Weiner explains, "acts on plants like a chemical fertilizer." Even so, no one knows if ever-increasing amounts of carbon dioxide in the atmosphere will tip the balance and prove instead to be chemical death for the plants.

Another more unpredictable feedback that supercomputers can't calculate is the impact of ash from volcanoes and meteors. We simply can't foretell when a major volcanic eruption or dust produced by a meteor will upset earth's temperature. Even the intensity of radiation from the sun is unpredictable. Another feedback the computers can't predict is soil moisture.

The human factor is difficult to predict, too. For example, chlorofluorocarbons (CFCs), which have been blamed for the ominous holes in earth's ozone layer, contribute some twenty percent to the greenhouse gases. Also, if the warm summers of the 1980s are any indication, it's possible that as the earth warms, humans will increase their use of carbon-dioxide producing fuels as the demand for electricity rises. The particles that pollution introduces into the air become the nuclei around which water vapor condenses, which give cities like Los Angeles and New York City their hazy, smoggy glow. Studies show that rainfall in areas affected by pollution increases. Yet this rain does not possess the life-giving qualities of water that we have come to expect.

Acid rain literally kills the lakes and streams it falls on in the northeastern United States, Canada, and Scandinavia. Acid rain forms when pollutants such as sulfur dioxide and nitrogen oxides combine with other gases and chemicals in the atmosphere to form sulfuric acid. In areas poor in natural alkaline rock, such as limestone, the acidity of the rain can't be neutralized.

Many lakes in the Adirondack Mountains, for example, are picture-postcard clean and clear. This is a sign, however ironic, that all life in the lake has died as a result of acid rain. Scientists note another form of acid rain from increasing amounts of methane in the upper level of the troposphere. Here, the methane reacts with chlorine and forms hydrochloric acid.

The tall smokestacks of heavy industry are responsible for acid rain. Fossil fuel-burning plants build smokestacks hundreds of (and sometimes more than one thousand) feet high to lift pollutants away from the area. The waste reaches into the atmosphere and is carried by winds thousands of miles around the globe, where it eventually falls to earth in the form of acid rain.

In addition to being unable to incorporate all of these feedbacks, global circulation models suffer from what scientists call coarse resolution. Each box in the model represents an area three hundred miles across and twenty miles high. This problem, along with the difficulty of factoring in all of earth's feedbacks, has produced widely differing predictions from each of the five models in use. According to _The New York Times_, the gradual impact of these variables is being studied by only one of the models at the Goddard Research Center. All the other models disregard the subtle feedback variables and their effects over time. Though each of the models doubles the amount of greenhouse gases, the results vary.

While the models have been useful in showing what the general impact of global warming would be, they are not able to predict the ramifications on the local level. Physicist and best-selling science writer John Gribbin explains the limitations of the circulation models in his book _The Hole in the Sky_: "As far as the computer is concerned, the temperature over all of Colorado is the same, while the cloud cover over Britain consists either of a uniform bank of cloud or of no cloud at all (some of the models do not even acknowledge the existence of such details as the British Isles)." The number of variables in predicting the earth's weather makes it unlikely that any computer now or in the near future could perform the many calculations necessary to encompass all the feedbacks in earth's complex weather system.

Ozone and CFCs

Another frightening aspect of the greenhouse problem is the recent discovery of holes in the ozone layer over the North and South poles. Composed of three oxygen atoms, ozone is destroyed when chlorofluorocarbons (CFCs) and halons react with ultraviolet light. The ultraviolet light breaks the CFCs apart, freeing chlorine (or bromine in halon) to steal one oxygen atom from the ozone (forming chlorine monoxide) and destroy the ozone. The process continues as the oxygen atom in the chlorine monoxide combines with another oxygen atom, leaving the chlorine free to destroy more ozone. In this way, just one chlorine atom can destroy as many as one hundred thousand ozone molecules.

While the hole in the ozone fluctuates from spring to fall, the overall effect is quite threatening to life on earth. NASA reports that in the north, the ozone layer has decreased by 1.7 to 3 percent annually, with 2.3 to 6.2 percent decreases during the winter months. Over the antarctic, the situation appears to be much worse. Here, the hole has been estimated to be about the size of the United States, and it continues to expand. Without the protection of the ozone layer, harmful ultraviolet rays reach earth, causing an increase in skin cancer and cataracts and harming human immune systems. At the base of the food chain, ocean phytoplankton also are harmed by ultraviolet light, which significantly reduces their rate of photosynthesis. Slowing them down could throw the entire food chain out of whack.

CFCs are the chemical compounds that revolutionized air conditioners, refrigerators, home insulation, cleaning solvents, and fire extinguishers. The link between CFCs and their harmful effects on the ozone was discovered during the early 1970s, and the United States and Canada responded by banning nonessential aerosols in 1978, with other developed countries following their lead. Even with the recent efforts to reduce the production of CFCs, we may be too late to save the ozone. As noted scientist Sayed Z. El-Sayed pointed out in *Natural History*, "The impending threats posed by stratospheric pollutants underscore the irony that, while governments plan to construct shields against nuclear missiles, the shield that protects us all from destructive ultraviolet radiation is threatened by man's own folly and shortsightedness." CFCs are long-lived, lasting to seventy-five and one hundred years, and may not be released into the atmosphere immediately, so it's unlikely, even with controls, that we can eradicate them from the atmosphere any time soon.

CFCs enter the atmosphere either during their manufacture or when they are discarded, though most CFCs are emitted when they are thrown out. Industry and the public show some resistance to stopping the use of CFCs, arguing that alternatives are presently too expensive to produce and may prove toxic in other ways. The economic stakes for the refrigerators, cars and trucks, supermarket cases, and commercial-building air conditioning units in the world are high. Sales of refrigerators and freezers in the United States alone total three billion dollars, and manufacturers predict higher prices with the use of alternative coolants and insulation. Others point out that in 1981, CFC manufacturers stopped researching alternatives. It wasn't until 1987, when the ozone crisis again commanded the public's attention, that industry resumed its research efforts.

At present, there are seven kinds of products that contain CFCs: closed cell foams, open cell foams, refrigeration materials, air conditioners and chillers, cleaning solvents, hospital sterilants, and fire extinguishers. All of these products enjoy widespread use; cutting back on CFCs is proving to be a political as well as an economic battle.

The closed and open cell foams contain CFC-11 and CFC-12, the CFCs that most damage the atmosphere. Closed cell foams, or rigid foams, include insulation; packing materials for fast-food restaurants and foamed trays on which meat, produce, and poultry are packed in stores; flotation devices; and insulation used in construction. Styrofoam cups also fall into this category, but have less CFC content than the others. This type of foam is also used as insulation in refrigerated trucks and in home refrigerators and freezers. These foams emit CFCs when they are thrown out and break apart. Open cell, or flexible foams, emit CFCs when they are produced. Flexible foams are used in items that need cushioning such as car upholstery, bedding, and carpet pads.

Home refrigerators and freezers contain another CFC, too. They are cooled with R-12 gas, more commonly known as Freon (Du Pont), Isotron (Penwalt Corporation), or Genetron (Allied-Signal Inc.). When a refrigerator or freezer is thrown out or repaired, the gas is allowed to leak out. Commercial refrigerators and freezers also contain gases like R-12 and contaminate the atmosphere when they are thrown out or repaired.

Automobile air conditioners, room air conditioners, and industrial chillers all use refrigerants made with CFCs. These, too, leak poison into the atmosphere when serviced or broken. The American automobile reigns supreme in accounting for three-quarters of all the CFC emissions from car air conditioners.

Mixtures of CFC gases are used to sterilize hospital instruments and to make presterilized equipment. Fire extinguishers contain halons, which are similar to CFCs. Extinguishers containing halons pump toxins into the air when they are used on the computer equipment, books, and other valuable goods that would be destroyed by water. Home extinguishers generally are made using dry chemicals and do not contain halons.

Nonetheless, given that in the United States, refrigerants pump forty-five percent of the CFCs into the atmosphere, blowing agents thirty percent, cleaning solvents twenty percent, and aerosols five percent, environmental groups are pushing for alternatives to CFCs where possible, and the recycling and reclamation of existing CFCs. The CFCs in refrigerators and air conditioners could be stored in "vampires" when the appliances are being repaired. There are also machines that can recycle contaminated refrigerants, which can be used again.

Healthy rain forests like this one in Trinidad are threatened by slash-and-burn deforestation. Deforestation occurs when countries want to make more land available for farming. It destroys many plant and animal species and often doesn't offer the bountiful farmland that was hoped for. In many places the soil is poor and will not support agricultural development.

WHAT WE'RE DOING

Though scientists have been warning us about the harmful effects of CFCs since the early 1970s, we have been slow to take steps to stem the tide of our destruction. It took the United Nations Environmental Program (UNEP) ten years to convince twenty-four countries to agree on regulating CFC production. Signed in 1987, the Montreal Protocol calls for a fifty percent reduction in the worldwide production of CFCs by 1999; it has now been signed by about fifty nations. Recently, the European Economic Community (EEC) called for a ban of all CFCs by 2000.

For the most part, industrialized nations are taking steps to respond to the ozone and greenhouse crisis. Developing nations, however, can't afford to experiment with technologies they are just beginning to use. Talks are underway to provide developing nations like China, India, South Korea, and Brazil with economic incentives to convert to CFC alternatives, but this could cost developed nations billions of dollars.

The International Council of Scientific Unions is planning an International Geosphere-Biosphere Program (IGBP) to research the changing climate. While the United States has pledged to research and implement programs affecting the global climate, research funds for 1989 were only $134 million, and conservation programs through the Department of Energy were budgeted only $166 million.

Still, some steps are being taken to minimize the impact of CFCs and other pollutants on the planet. The plastics industry has begun looking into alternatives to CFCs and has begun a recycling program. While less than one percent of all plastics are recycled, the Plastics Recycling Foundation, composed of forty-five companies, has asked the Center for Plastics Recycling Research at Rutgers University to develop a recycling system that is already being used commercially. On the local level, recycling of all wastes is getting a stronger push than ever. Yet the Environmental Protection Agency is hard-pressed to adequately monitor the effects of pollution on the planet. In other sectors observing the greenhouse effect, researchers are hampered by the location of most weather stations on land, which leaves out the oceans, making a truly global perspective impossible. Satellites planned for launch in the 1990s could fill in some of the gaps in our research. In the meantime, NASA launched the *NOAA-11* satellite in 1988, which will monitor the destruction of the ozone layer for two to five years.

Clouds appear to be different colors depending on the density and composition of the particles of which they are made and the angle at which sunlight hits them.

WHAT ABOUT THE FUTURE?

The growing hysteria over the condition of planet earth leads many to wonder if our concern is more for ourselves than for the planet. After all, earth has survived age after age of climate change without the help or hindrance of humans. As John Gribbin expresses it in _The Hole in the Sky_:

_We_ think that it would be a disaster if humankind were wiped off the face of the Earth. But look at it another way. Today, humankind is busily destroying the tropical forests that are the core of Gaia; we are changing the climate through the greenhouse effect; and we are destroying ozone in large quantities....These effects add up to a disaster for other forms of life on Earth, as great as the extinctions that occurred 65 million years ago. From the "point of view" of Gaia, the destruction of humankind might well be a good thing.

Whether or not our efforts to monitor and correct earth's changing climate are motivated by self-interest or by a respect for the life (and other life forms) of the planet itself, we must take responsibility for the destruction our "superior" technology has wrought.

Grass-roots community recycling programs and activism and the political response of nations the world over are just a beginning. The media have taken up the cause, as exemplified in daily reports in newspapers and on television. _Time_ even named earth the "Planet of the Year" in January 1989, devoting an entire issue to earth's endangered state. Our hope lies in continuing to recognize that the weather is intimately connected with our survival on this planet. As long as we continue to demand political and industrial solutions to environmental problems, there is hope that our children will not define "nature" as a separate entity but as a living being of which we are all a part. When we can do that, we surely will have taken the first step toward environmental health and harmony.

Sources

ENVIRONMENT

GOVERNMENT AGENCIES

ENVIRONMENTAL PROTECTION AGENCY
Enforcement and Compliance Monitoring
401 M Street, SW
Washington, DC 20460

NATIONAL OCEANIC AND ATMOSPHERIC
ADMINISTRATION
(Commerce Department)
14th Street & Constitution Avenue, NW
Washington, DC 20230
202-377-3436

NATIONAL ENVIRONMENTAL SATELLITE,
DATA, AND INFORMATION SERVICE
Federal Building 4
Suitland, MD 20233
202-763-7190

OCEAN ASSESSMENTS
11400 Rockville Pike
Rockville, MD 20852
202-443-8933

SENATE ENVIRONMENT AND PUBLIC
WORKS COMMITTEE
Subcommittee on Environmental Protection
SH-408
Washington, DC 20510
202-224-6691

PUBLIC INTEREST GROUPS

EARTH ISLAND INSTITUTE
300 Broadway, Suite 28
San Francisco, CA 94133
415-788-3666

ENVIRONMENTAL DEFENSE FUND
257 Park Avenue South
New York, NY 10010
212-505-2100

ENVIRONMENTAL POLICY INSTITUTE
218 D Street, SE
Washington, DC 20003
202-544-2600

FRIENDS OF THE EARTH
218 D Street, SE
Washington, DC 20003
202-543-4312

GREENPEACE
1436 U Street, NW
Washington, DC 20009
202-462-1177

NATURAL RESOURCES DEFENSE COUNCIL
122 East 42nd Street
New York, NY 10168

THE NATURE CONSERVANCY
1815 N. Lynn Street
Arlington, VA 22209
708-841-5300

SIERRA CLUB
730 Polk Street
San Francisco, CA 94109

408 C Street, NE
Washington, DC 20002
202 547-1141

WORLDWATCH INSTITUTE
1776 Massachusetts Avenue, NW
Washington, DC 20036
202-452-1999

RESEARCH CENTERS

SCRIPPS INSTITUTION OF
OCEANOGRAPHY
University of California at San Diego
A-033B
La Jolla, CA 92093

SMITHSONIAN ENVIRONMENTAL
RESEARCH CENTER
(Smithsonian Institution)
P.O. Box 28
Contees Wharf Road
Edgewater, MD 21037
301-798-4424

WOODS HOLE OCEANOGRAPHIC INSTI-
TUTION
Woods Hole, MA 02543
508-548-1400

WEATHER

GOVERNMENT AGENCIES

NATIONAL OCEANIC AND ATMOSPHERIC
ADMINISTRATION
(Commerce Department)
National Climate Program
11400 Rockville Pike
Rockville, MD 20852
301-443-8646

NATIONAL CLIMATE CENTER
Federal Building
Asheville, NC 28801

NATIONAL SEVERE STORMS FORECAST
CENTER
Federal Building
Kansas City, MO 64106

NATIONAL WEATHER SERVICE
8060 13th Street
Silver Spring, MD 20910
301-427-7622
(see your telephone directory for local
offices)

NATIONAL WEATHER SERVICE
National Meteorological Center
5200 Auth Road
Camp Springs, MD
mailing address: Washington DC 20233
301-763-8016

NATIONAL SCIENCE FOUNDATION
Atmospheric Sciences, Room 644
1800 G Street, NW
Washington, DC 20550
202-357-9874

NON-GOVERNMENT AGENCIES

AMERICAN ASSOCIATION FOR THE
ADVANCEMENT OF SCIENCE
International Science
1333 H Street, NW
Washington, DC 20005
202-326-6650

AMERICAN METEOROLOGICAL SOCIETY
45 Beacon Street
Boston, MA 02108
617-227-2425

NATIONAL CENTER FOR ATMOSPHERIC
RESEARCH
P.O. Box 3000
Boulder, CO 80307

NATIONAL WEATHER ASSOCIATION
4400 Stamp Road, Suite 404
Temple Hills, MD 20748
301-899-3784

ROYAL METEOROLOGICAL SOCIETY
James Glaisher House,
Grenville Place
Bracknell, Berkshire RG12 1BX England
WEATHER MODIFICATION ASSOCIATION
P.O. Box 8116
Fresno, CA 93727

WORLD METEOROLOGICAL ORGANIZA
TION
Caisse postale № 5
CH-1211 Geneva 20
Switzerland

Further Reading

Books

Brown, Michael H. *The Toxic Cloud*. New York: Perennial/Harper and Row, 1987.

Carson, Rachel. *Silent Spring*. Boston: Houghton Mifflin, 1962.

Gribbin, John, Ralph Hardy, Peter Wright, and John Kington. *The Weather Book*. Boston: Little, Brown and Company, 1982.

Ludlum, David M. *The Weather Factor (An Amazing Collection of Little-Known Facts About How the Weather Has Influenced the American Scene from Colonial to Modern Times)*. Boston: Houghton Mifflin Company, 1984.

Schaefer, Vincent J. and John A.. Day. *A Field Guide to the Atmosphere*. (The Peterson Field Guide Series). Boston: Houghton Mifflin Company, 1981.

Schneider, Stephen H. and Randi Londer. *The Coevolution of Climate and Life*. San Francisco: Sierra Club Books, 1984.

Trefil, James S. *Meditations at Sunset: A Scientist Looks at the Sky*. New York: Collier Books, Macmillan Publishing Company, 1987.

Weiner, Jonathan. *Planet Earth*. New York: Bantam Books, 1986.

Young, Louise B. *Earth's Aura*. New York: Alfred A. Knopf, Inc., 1977.

Periodicals

Daily Weather Maps
U.S. Government Printing Office
Washington, DC 20402

Monthly and Seasonal Weather Outlook
U.S. Government Printing Office
Washington, DC 20402

Science News
1719 N Street, NW
Washington, DC 20036

Weatherwise
Heldref Publications
4000 Albemarle Street, NW
Washington, DC 20016

WMO Bulletin
World Meteorological Organization
Caisse postale № 5
CH-1211 Geneva 20 Switzerland

PHOTO CREDITS

© Ablinger/Photri: 51 top

© Alpha/FPG International: 112

© S. Back/Daily Telegraph/International Stock Photos: 71

© F.J. Baker/Marvin Dembinsky Photo Associates: 97

© Paulette Brunner/Tom Stack & Associates: 22-23

© Mike Chuang/FPG International: 20-21

© Sharon Cummings/Marvin Dembinsky Photo Associates: 29 left

© Daily Telegraph/International Stock Photos: 74-75

© Marvin Dembinsky Photo Associates: 6-7, 8-9, 44, 109

© Dick Dietrich Photography: 90-91, 125

© Chad Ehlers/International Stock Photos: 60-61

© Gerry Ellis/Ellis Wildlife: 38-39, 116-117, 118-119

© Warren Faidley/NOAA: 86-87

© Lee Foster/FPG International: 43

© Dave Gleiter/Visual Horizons/FPG International: 66

© S. Gottlieb/FPG International: 12-13

© Ron Goulet/Marvin Dembinsky Photo Associates: 18-19

© Tom & Michele Grimm/International Stock Photos: 77

© Hansen/FPG International: 32

© Kermit Johnson/International Stock Photos: 123

© M.P. Kahl/FPG International: 36 bottom

© Konran Media Inc./FPG International: 42

© Maurice & Sally Landre/FPG International: 110-111

© F. Lazi/FPG International: 16-17

© Gerard Lemmo/FPG International: 88-89, 100

© Mike Magnuson: 48-49, 53, 62-63, 120

© Skip Moody/Marvin Dembinsky Photo Associates: 55 left

© Jeffry W. Myers/FPG International: 106

© Edmund Nagele/FPG International: 46-47

© NASA/FPG International: 24-25, 31, 87 right

North Wind Picture Archives: 18, 50, 65, 80, 81, 82, 83, 84, 102-103

© Stan Osolinski/Marvin Dembinsky Photo Associates: 14-15, 29 right, 45, 52-53 top, 55 right, 94, 97, 98-99

© Photri: 72-73, 78-79, 85

© Jim Pickerell/FPG International: 36 top

© Terry Qing/FPG International: 68-69

© Ted Reuther/Marvin Dembinsky Photo Associates: 26-27

© Carl R. Sams II/Marvin Dembinsky Photo Associates: 28 right

© Ken Scott/Marvin Dembinsky Photo Associates: 28 left, 35, 52-53 bottom

© John Scowan/FPG International: 56-57

© Clyde H. Smith/FPG International: 11

© J.S. Sroka/Marvin Dembinsky Photo Associates: 57

© Jean F. Stoick/Marvin Dembinsky Photo Associates: 41

© Fiona Sunquist/Tom Stack & Associates: 113

© Wim Swaan/FPG International: 104-105

© J. Sylvester/FPG International: 76

© Renaud Thomas/FPG International: 58-59

© Visual Horizons/FPG International: 93 right

© P. Wallick/FPG International: 40

All illustrations by Mary Moriarty except page 54 by Anne Meskey.